Dealing with
the Russians

Dealing with the Russians

Andrew Monaghan

polity

The right of Andrew Monaghan to be identified as Author of this Work has been asserted in accordance with the UK Copyright, Designs and Patents Act 1988.

First published in 2019 by Polity Press

Polity Press
65 Bridge Street
Cambridge CB2 1UR, UK

Polity Press
101 Station Landing
Suite 300
Medford, MA 02155, USA

ISBN-13: 978-1-5095-2761-8
ISBN-13: 978-1-5095-2762-5 (pb)

A catalogue record for this book is available from the British Library.

Library of Congress Cataloging-in-Publication Data

Names: Monaghan, Andrew, Dr, author.
Title: Dealing with the Russians / Andrew Monaghan.
Description: Medford, MA : Polity, 2019. | Includes bibliographical references and index.
Identifiers: LCCN 2018043365 (print) | LCCN 2018054118 (ebook) | ISBN 9781509527656 (Epub) | ISBN 9781509527618 (hardback) | ISBN 9781509527625 (pbk.)
Subjects: LCSH: Western countries–Foreign relations–Russia (Federation) | Russia (Federation)–Foreign relations–Western countries. | Russia (Federation)–Strategic aspects. | Russia (Federation)–Military policy | National security–European Union countries. | National security–United States. | Security, International.
Classification: LCC D2025.5.R8 (ebook) | LCC D2025.5.R8 M64 2019 (print) | DDC 327.470182/1–dc23
LC record available at https://lccn.loc.gov/2018043365

Typeset in 11 on 13 pt Sabon by Toppan Best-set Premedia Limited
Printed and bound in the UK by TJ International Limited

For further information on Polity, visit our website: politybooks.com

Contents

Abbreviations

A2/AD	Anti-Access/Area Denial
ABM	Anti-Ballistic Missile (Treaty)
BMD	Ballistic Missile Defence
CAATSA	Countering America's Adversaries Through Sanctions Act
CCW	Changing Character of War Centre
CFE	(Treaty on) Conventional Forces in Europe
CJEF	Combined Joint Expeditionary Force
DASKAA	Defending American Security from Kremlin Aggression Act
eFP	enhanced Forward Presence
EU	European Union
GDP	gross domestic product
GPV	State Armaments Programme
IMF	International Monetary Fund
INF	Intermediate-Range Nuclear Forces (Treaty)
JEF	Joint Expeditionary Force
KGB	Committee of State Security
NATO	North Atlantic Treaty Organization
NRC	NATO–Russia Council
RAP	Readiness Action Plan
SACEUR	Supreme Allied Commander Europe

START	Strategic Arms Reduction Treaty
UN	United Nations
USSR	Union of Soviet Socialist Republics
VJTF	Very High Readiness Joint Task Force
VPK	*Voenno-Promyshlenni Kurier*
WoTR	*War on the Rocks*
WPA	Website of the Presidential Administration of Russia

Preface and Acknowledgements

The 'Decline of the West' – and the Emergence of a Russian Challenge

Until 2014, the idea of major, great-power war in modern Europe had become so unthinkable that it did not feature in discussion, even in fiction. Events that year in Ukraine changed all that. The language of war has returned to European politics, and officials and observers have begun to reflect on what it might look like. Euro-Atlantic officials and observers began to talk informally of the 'Eastern front', and the 'threat from the East'. In the media, documentaries have been screened debating the 'return of old enemies', even the eruption of World War III, and the conditions under which nuclear weapons might be used in the case of a Russian invasion of North Atlantic Treaty Organization (NATO) member states.[1]

The war in Ukraine broke out at a time when the Euro-Atlantic community had long been suffering a crisis of confidence. The impact of the financial crisis of 2008 and subsequent slow growth and prolonged economic austerity policies, the high-profile failures in Iraq and the problematic interventions in Libya and Syria have all contributed to an accelerating sense of weakness and an ebbing of the post-Cold War era, 'End of History' confidence.

Indeed, it has been a commonplace for some years to argue that the international liberal order is under threat from internal and external challenges. Sustained domestic political and economic uncertainty, combined with resurgent authoritarian powers, have meant that Western liberalism is seen to be in retreat, even 'under siege' – not only are the countries that built the liberal order weaker today than they have been for seventy years, but, according to the *Financial Times*'s Edward Luce, since the year 2000, twenty-five democracies have failed, 'including three in Europe – Russia, Turkey and Hungary'. The 'West's crisis is real, structural and likely to persist', he lamented.[2]

This is part of a wider debate about a 'post-American world', the decline of the West, the 'rise of the rest' and the shift of power to the East.[3] Richard Haass, a former diplomat and now the president of the influential US think tank the Council on Foreign Relations, is among those who have argued that 'centrifugal forces' are gaining the upper hand, and there is a shrinking American ability to translate its considerable power into influence.[4] And as one prominent journalist put it, the West's 'centuries long domination of world affairs is now coming to a close', and with the growing concentration of wealth in Asia, the West is losing its ability to function as a pole of stability and power imposing order on a chaotic world. Thus Gideon Rachman stated that the 'crumbling of the Western dominated world order' has increased the chance of conflict not just in East Asia but in the Middle East and Eastern Europe.[5] This discussion has provided fertile ground for other debates about the decline of US and Western power and the challenges it faces, the rise of other powers and the possibility of this leading to war.[6]

The loss of confidence has two main roots. First, as John Bew, Professor of History and Foreign Policy at King's College London, put it, there have been 'profound failures' in the Anglo-American world's ability to anticipate, understand and come to terms with the complex problems it has encountered in other countries and regions. These 'shortcomings have contributed to a sense of loss of control, of being at the mercy of events and a general loss of authority in world affairs'.[7] Reminding us that concerns about world order have permeated Anglo-American foreign policy thinking for over a century, Bew argues that they are simultaneously forward-looking, aspirational expressions of the desire to give the international system a destination point made in one's own image, and yet riddled with inescapable 'Spenglerian angst', the sense of 'civilizational vulnerability, sharpened by periods of technological change, fiercer international competition or confrontation with "The Other" from different parts of the world'.[8]

And ours is indeed seen as a state of permanent crisis, an 'age of anxiety', an 'unprecedented condition of vulnerability' and connectedness that makes the United States and its allies increasingly open to violent threats. Patrick Porter, Professor of International Security and Strategy at the University of Birmingham, has argued that the US, which ought to be one of the most secure states in history, is perpetually *insecure*, due to fears about the revolutions in communications, transport and weapons technology that have served to reduce frontiers and make the world dangerously small. US security is thus implicated everywhere, and this notion of insecurity in a shrunken world has lain behind the development since the early 2000s of a series of policies including pre-emptive war in the name of anticipatory defence, and other measures such as the development of the Ballistic Missile Defence programme (BMD).[9]

The second root is quantitative, reflecting concern about a sense of loss of material power. If China and Russia are seen to pose the main challenges to the 'relatively peaceful and prosperous' international order, the 'combined military power' of the US and its allies has served as the 'greatest check' on their ambitions.[10] But as the BBC's Mark Urban argued in 2015, a series of long-term trends, including declining defence spending (from 2012 to 2014, thirteen of the twenty fastest-declining defence budgets were in Europe), mean that there is a 'qualitative as well as quantitative erosion' of Western superiority. 'The edge, the Western advantage and along with that the ability to deter people in parts of the world from doing desperate things, is going – if it has not already disappeared.'[11] A year later, a leaked British Army report suggested that, on the basis of lessons learnt from the war in Ukraine, Russia 'currently has a significant capability edge over UK force elements', and NATO allies were 'scrambling to catch up'.[12]

Then in 2018, launching the new US National Defence Strategy, US Secretary of Defense James Mattis used much the same language when he stated that 'our competitive edge has eroded in every domain of warfare – air, land, sea, space, and cyber space – and it is continuing to erode'. He argued that fast technological change and the long-running wars the US had waged had diminished US military capabilities: US armed forces had to cope with 'inadequate and misaligned resources'. Mattis emphasized that great-power competition was now the main focus of US security, and that the 'unipolar moment in which the US was the only superpower is no longer with us'.[13]

An important feature of the concern about the international order being in retreat is a widespread view that the post-Cold War goal of a Europe 'whole, free and at peace' is under threat. If the range of challenges is seen to be broad, from Brexit to migration, many see Russia to be one of the most prominent. As one US commentator has put it, Russia, 'fresh from perpetrating the first violent annexation of territory on the European continent since World War II, forges on with a dizzying military buildup and casually talks about the use of battlefield nuclear weapons against NATO member states'.[14] Along with many others, James Kirchick suggested that Russia was the most important of these threats because of the way that it supported and magnified the others. It is such a widely held view that he is worth quoting at length:

As Europe's political stability, social cohesion, economic prosperity and security are more threatened today than at any point since the Cold War, Russia is destabilizing the Continent on every front. ... Fomenting European disintegration from within, Russia also threatens Europe from without through its massive military buildup, frequent intimidation of NATO members and efforts to overturn the continent's security architecture by weakening the transatlantic link with America.[15]

After many years of prolonged neglect in which Russia was not a priority, the shock of the annexation of Crimea and the war in Eastern Ukraine catapulted Russia to the forefront of the Euro-Atlantic policy agenda. Perhaps belatedly, the crisis emphasized for many that Russia was no longer a partner, but a challenger. It also generated much debate about what Putin would do next – was Crimea just the beginning of a new expansionist policy? – and the sources of Moscow's actions.

Some, such as Michael McFaul, an academic who also served as US Ambassador to Moscow from 2012 to 2014, frame the current crisis in immediate causes. Acknowledging that the questions of great-power competition and international order and US policies play a role, McFaul emphasizes instead the roles of Russian domestic policies and particularly the return of Vladimir Putin to the Russian presidency in 2012 as being the key factors in the current crisis.[16]

But there is little consensus. Others put it into a longer-term historical context of 'typical Russian activity'. James Clapper, former US Director of National Intelligence, for instance, asserted that Russian interference in the US election was 'just the historical practices of the Russians, who typically, almost genetically driven to co-opt, penetrate, gain favour, whatever, which is a typical Russian technique' (sic).[17] Others point to traditional Russian imperialism: Russia is 'following in the footsteps of its historical predecessors and will continue to do so because of similar ideological, cultural security and geopolitical drivers'.[18]

Still others highlight a different dynamic. If some frame
the Ukraine crisis as being the result of a dynamic interaction between the Euro-Atlantic community and Russia, a
negative-sum game,[19] others have argued that the crisis
erupted because of US policy failures that squandered an
opportunity for better relations,[20] and because Russia has
begun to respond more forcefully to US policy. Though
they do not all agree on the balance of blame, such observers place the current deterioration in relations in the post-
Cold War context – one of a longer-term, deepening divide
between the Euro-Atlantic community and Russia, and the
failure to reach a lasting settlement after the Cold War.
According to Richard Sakwa, Professor of Russian and
European Politics at the University of Kent, therefore, the
'competing narratives about the end of the Cold War are
grounded in a profound interpretative gulf about the nature
of the international system', and there is a strategic impasse
between the Euro-Atlantic community and Russia.[21]

With the persistent deterioration in relations, each year
seemingly showing a 'new low' in relations, the thrust of
much of the debate has been about the emergence of a
return to 'Cold War type' relations between the West and
Russia. There has been much criticism about the failure of
the Euro-Atlantic community to stop Russia and the specific
policies that it could implement, with most emphasis on
the need to deter and contain Russia.[22]

What does seem clear, however, is that the Euro-Atlantic
community's relationship with Russia has entered a new
era – moving beyond the 'post-Cold War' era of what could
be called 'Russian democracy embattled' into 'Russia as
challenger'. The precise character of this shift has been
obscured by an important ambiguity. On the one hand,
there are numerous deeply entrenched questions that encourage a strong sense of only glacial movement in Russian
politics, foreign policy and relations with the Euro-Atlantic
community. There is much repetition in the debate about
the relationship, with a strong sense of déjà vu about the
core questions – the (un)sustainability of Putin's leadership

and Russia's long term decline, and the many disagreements about Euro-Atlantic security, particularly the debate about NATO's supposed 'no-enlargement promise'. Officials and observers who have recently returned to Russia-watching after a substantial break occasionally lament how familiar the discussion all looks.

On the other hand, since 2014 the pace of events has seemed to accelerate as the relationship has lurched from crisis to crisis, and from one panic about Russian action to the next. Not only does the debate become more partisan, it has also moved into new subjects, such as election interference and cyber security and Russian actions in Syria. Each new feature shapes the policy debate about Russia, driving it further into the realms of security.

The development of this book reflects this trajectory. When it was originally conceived in 2016, partly to respond to the repetitions and abstractions of yet another round of debate about a 'new Cold War' and the emergence of debate about so-called 'Russian hybrid warfare', and partly to emphasize the need to see dialogue and deterrence not as ends in themselves but as the consequences of a broader grand strategy, dialogue formed a larger proportion of the Euro-Atlantic community's intentions. And while it might reasonably be argued that with each crisis dialogue became ever more important, with each crisis the possibilities for dialogue simultaneously narrowed and receded.

The attempted murder, in March 2018 in Salisbury, of the former Russian military intelligence officer Sergei Skripal and his daughter appears to have had significant and ongoing consequences for relations between the Euro-Atlantic community and Russia. It resulted not just in London accusing the Russian authorities of direct involvement, but in large numbers of expulsions of diplomats and intelligence officers from across the Euro-Atlantic community and beyond (with Russia reciprocating), and in a second suspension of high-level dialogue in four years. In August that year, the US imposed sanctions against Russia for using chemical or biological weapons in violation of international law or against its own nationals. For their part, the British authorities publicly named two men as suspects, charging them with conspiracy to murder, attempted murder, causing grievous bodily harm and the possession and use of a nerve agent, novichok, contrary to the Chemical Weapons Act. Though the UK did not immediately apply to Russia for their extradition, the British authorities have obtained European Arrest Warrants and an Interpol Red Notice for the two men, believed to be Russian military intelligence officers travelling under the aliases Alexander Petrov and Ruslan Boshirov. According to one northern (non-British) European politician, the events have resulted in a different atmosphere: 'politically, all hopes of a better relationship stopped with Salisbury'.[23]

Not for the first time, therefore, there is a need to reflect on first principles, diagnosis of the problem and both the wider picture and the longer trajectory of relations with Russia. This book brings together history, politics, policy and strategy not so much to make specific policy recommendations about how to 'deal with the Russians' today and tomorrow, but to step back to make a bigger argument for a broader shift in terms of conceiving the nature of the challenge Russia poses. This requires returning to the roots of questions as much as setting out a path ahead.

Acknowledgements

If the idea of the book took shape in 2016, it was written in the first half of 2018, and many debts of gratitude have accrued, as I have benefitted from much support from colleagues, friends and family. My colleagues at the Oxford Changing Character of War Centre (CCW), particularly Robert Johnson, Liz Robson, Graham Fairclough, Melissa Skorka, Chris Holloway and Ruth Murray, have been patient and supportive, notably during the final months of finishing the book, and have throughout offered help and timely and constructive advice. Additionally, I would like to thank

Pembroke College, Oxford, and the Axel and Margaret Ax:son Johnson Foundation for Public Benefit for their generous support of CCW's work, and especially the Russia and Northern European Defence and Security project.

At the heart of the book are the many interviews and discussions I have had with politicians, officials and military personnel in the UK, the US, across NATO and the European Union (EU), and Russia. Though such discussions must remain anonymous, I am grateful for the time you have spent with me. I would like to thank the audiences of three lectures at which I presented these ideas, including in Washington, Oxford and London, for their questions and insightful comments. I am indebted to two anonymous reviewers for Polity who gave detailed and thoughtful comments on the draft. Likewise, friends have taken the trouble to discuss the themes of the book at length, even going so far as to read and comment on parts of, or all of, the draft. Among them are Nazrin Mehdiyeva, Richard Connolly, Julian Cooper, Silvana Malle, Dov Lynch and Robert Dover. They not only have offered constructive critique of this particular book, but are ever ready with their friendship and support. The thinking that influenced the book is also the product of many years of discussions with friends, including Florence Gaub and Henry Plater-Zyberk. Thank you. In Russia, as always, I would like to thank Boris Mikhailovich and Mikhail Borisovich and Ekaterina Vladimirovna for their kindness and support. The work of IA, PL, and, particularly during the writing of this book, IK, FEC and PAT has played an important role: you are remembered.

I am grateful for the help of several librarians, particularly Simon Blundell, and also David Bates and his team at Chatham House. Thanks are also due to Antulio J. Echevaria II and Nora Ellis of the *Parameters* journal for permission to reuse and build on material first published in the article 'The "War" in Russia's "Hybrid Warfare"'.

Similarly, much gratitude is due to Louise Knight, Nekane Tanaka Galdos, Sophie Wright and their colleagues at Polity for their patience, encouragement and editorial attentiveness throughout the process. Their positive approach from the early discussions through to the final text has been essential. Thank you!

Most of all, my thanks and love go to my family, Charles and Dorothy and Yulia, for their kindness, generosity, patience and encouragement. How lucky I am. With your support and love, this book and so much else has been and is made possible. So the book is dedicated to you, and to Lara Andreevna, whose happy presence continues as a guiding light to what is really important in life.

Andrew Monaghan, June 2018

1

The Predicament

How to deal with Russia? This question has become ever more urgent since Russia's annexation of Crimea in early 2014. Senior Western politicians and officials frequently condemn Russian actions in robust terms, and states and international organizations have published official documents naming Russia as a rival, as aggressive and defining itself in opposition to the West.[1] The USA and European Union (EU) sought to punish Russian actions and change Russian policy by suspending Moscow's participation in mechanisms for dialogue, such as the G8, and imposing financial and economic sanctions on Russia, whilst emphasizing their own collective defence and deterrence measures. Despite the rhetoric and the policies, though, Moscow has not altered course. Indeed, the Russian leadership has vehemently rejected Western accusations, introduced counter-sanctions and increased the number and size of its own military exercises, including near North Atlantic Treaty Organization (NATO) borders.

A sense of the rapid emergence of competing, even opposing camps has become ever more explicit, with both sides emphasizing the loss of trust in the relationship and accusing the other of the responsibility for initiating and then escalating the tensions and increasing military activity both in specific areas such as the Baltic Sea and Syria, and beyond. Numerous close encounters illustrate the tension and concern about the possibility for accidental escalation.

The dangerous nature of the situation was made clear in November 2015, when Turkey shot down a Russian Su-24, an act which Russian Prime Minister Dmitri Medvedev claimed gave Moscow legitimate grounds to go to war. Noting that such direct attacks on states in the twentieth century led to war, he suggested that Turkey, through its act of aggression against Russia, had violated international norms, giving a '*casus belli*'. But in the present situation, he suggested, a 'war is the worst that could happen', and that's why a decision was taken not to give a 'symmetrical answer to what the Turks had done'.[2] Since then, there have been numerous similarly tense moments in Syria.

Russia's Emergence as a Peer Challenger

Russia is now seen by many in the Euro-Atlantic community to pose a significant threat to international security, and to be undermining the rules-based system. Many have argued, for instance, that Moscow uses so-called 'hybrid warfare' to challenge the cohesion and unity of NATO and the EU and the sovereignty of their member states, particularly Estonia, Latvia, Lithuania and Poland. 'Russian hybrid warfare', which is examined in more depth in chapter 2, is understood as conflict-related insecurity, a strategy, according to one prominent Western thinker, to 'confuse us and perplex us by not telling the truth' and disorient us about Vladimir Putin's intentions.[3] This has generated much talk of Moscow using 'asymmetric means' and 'measures short of war'.

In this vein, many accuse Moscow of interfering in the domestic politics of Euro-Atlantic states, of funding anti-EU political parties such as the French National Front, of interfering in the UK's referendum on its membership of the EU, and of spending millions 'to spread its version of reality in Europe, including sometimes fabrications'.[4] Indeed, such accusations spread across Europe, including Germany, the Czech Republic and Spain, with some suggesting that Russian hackers and trolls tried to increase support for separatism in Catalonia in 2017. And most prominent of all, of course, are the accusations of Russian interference in the US presidential elections in November 2016.[5] According to Joe Biden, US Vice President until 2017, therefore, the Russian government is 'brazenly assaulting the foundations of Western Democracy around the world … it has sought to weaken and subvert Western democracies from the inside by weaponizing information, cyberspace, energy and corruption'.[6]

Numerous senior British politicians and officials have also pointed to what they see as a Russian threat. In a prominent speech in November 2017, Prime Minister Theresa May accused Russia of threatening international order, 'fomenting conflict', repeatedly violating the national airspace of several European countries and mounting a sustained 'campaign of cyber espionage and disruption'.[7] The UK's Secretary of Defence asserted in December 2017 that Russia was at war with the UK, and then in January 2018 that Russia was seeking ways to damage the UK's economy by attacking its infrastructure, which could create 'total chaos and cause thousands and thousands of deaths'. He reiterated similar claims in February, noting that the UK had 'entered a new era of warfare' with Russian cyber attacks.[8]

Many also accuse Russia of indirectly and directly exacerbating the security challenges Europe faces. Philip Breedlove, then NATO's Supreme Allied Commander Europe (SACEUR), accused Russia of deliberately bombarding civilian centres in Syria to exacerbate the refugee crisis to 'overwhelm European structures and break European resolve'.[9] Equally, others see Russia as posing a direct military challenge to NATO, and putting itself on a 'collision course' with the alliance, particularly in terms of a possible Russian invasion of the Baltic states.[10]

Indeed, the use by the Russian leadership of military power to achieve policy ends has come as a shock to Euro-Atlantic officials and politicians. Many – including senior military figures – have been unpleasantly surprised by Russian military capabilities. In June 2016, the then commander of the US Army Europe, Lieutenant General Ben Hodges, pointed to the speed and scale of Russian capabilities: 'the Russians are able to move huge formations and lots of equipment a long distance, very fast', he noted. 'It's concerning', he suggested, because NATO does not have such speed. Hodges also pointed to comparative shortfalls in intelligence, surveillance, reconnaissance, short-range air defence and combat aviation.[11] The Russian 'Zapad-2017' exercises in autumn 2017 generated something approaching panic in Western media, as observers – supported in some instances by official assessments – estimated that the exercises would be over 100,000 strong and could be a cover for an invasion of the Baltic states or of Ukraine.[12] Even after the exercise was completed, prominent media sources quoted Western officials to suggest that Zapad had been a rehearsal for a 'full-scale conventional war' against NATO and the capture of the Baltic states, and a shock campaign against Germany and the Netherlands, Poland and Norway, as well as neutral Sweden and Finland.[13]

There is even concern in the US. General Joseph Dunford, then nominee chairman of the US joint chiefs of staff, told the Senate Armed Services Committee in July 2015 that Russia could pose an 'existential threat' to the US and that its behaviour was 'alarming'. Subsequently, in spring 2016, he stated that the 'Russian military presents the greatest array of threats to US interests'.[14] Others, including General Mark Milley, then Chief of Staff of the US Army, have agreed, stating that Russia should be considered the number one threat to the US because of its capabilities and intent. In November 2015, Milley stated that the situation with Russia is 'serious and growing more serious. I see Russia as aggressive, not just assertive. They attacked Georgia, they illegally seized Crimea, they have attacked Ukraine

... I would say that Russia's recent behaviour is adversarial to the interest of the US.'[15] Later, he stated his belief that Russia has an advantage in some military systems such that the US army is 'technically outranged and outgunned' by Russian ground-based direct or indirect fire systems, tanks and artillery.[16]

The Dual Dilemma

Within a short time, therefore, Western thinking about Euro-Atlantic security has undergone a substantial reactive evolution, with the result that, at least in regional terms, Russia is seen to be well on the way to becoming a near-peer or peer military competitor to NATO, and even the US. The sense of insecurity is palpable. Indeed, officials have noted that relations are in a 'vicious spiral from which it is difficult to extricate ourselves'.[17] Others have argued that there is a 'profound mutual insecurity', that relations reflect a 'security dilemma', in which 'each side sees the other side's efforts to improve its security as coming at its own expense', and leading to a cycle of increasing security measures that only heighten tension and insecurity.[18]

This sense of an emergent security dilemma frames the situation well, but requires elaboration. A security dilemma comes from actual and potential conflict, and reflects the (difficult) measurement of relative power, the subjective appraisal of defence sufficiency and potential threat. Cooperation to address this cycle of increasing security measures and escalating competition is rendered difficult because of the uncertainty in international affairs, and because all fear being betrayed by the other side – and thus left vulnerable. A security dilemma becomes especially complex when states cannot signal defensive intent because their defensive and offensive military forces are largely identical, and if offensive operations are deemed to be more effective than defensive ones – encouraging pre-emptive war in the case of political crisis.[19] All of this is relevant to the current relationship between the Euro-Atlantic community and Russia.

But there are two complicating points. First, as Michael Kofman, a research scientist at the Center for Naval Analysis in Washington, DC, has pointed out, there is no sudden major militarization on NATO's borders. While it is true that Russia has announced the (re-)creation of the 1st Guards Tank Army and other divisions, he notes, these units are only taking shape – like NATO's Very High Readiness Joint Task Force (VJTF), he suggested, they are aspirationally named. Furthermore, while NATO has Russia on its mind, Moscow is thinking about contingencies in Ukraine and Belarus.[20]

Second, according to the academics Ken Booth and Nicholas Wheeler, a security dilemma is a *two-level* predicament: first, a dilemma of interpretation and then, once this is resolved, a dilemma of response. They further define in a more detailed way the two stages of interpretation and response. A security *challenge* is a situation in which the dilemma of interpretation has been settled: this is only a dilemma of response. Finally, when leaders 'resolve their dilemma of response in a manner that creates a spiral of mutual hostility', this is a security *paradox*. Importantly, they note that one state's dilemma of response creates another's dilemma of interpretation, and so a spiral is created. By making the dilemma and paradox synonymous, Booth and Wheeler argue, we fail to find the core of the predicament.[21]

In these terms, then, the current situation does not appear to be a security dilemma. Rather, it appears as a *security challenge*, since for many, the dilemma of interpretation is already broadly resolved – Russia as an expansionist threat – with the dilemma of response yet to be resolved. The tension in relations is having a polarizing effect, dividing those who advocate the need for détente and to re-engage Russia in dialogue, and those who assert the need to reinforce deterrence against Russian aggression.

Those who argue for détente with Russia seek to prevent further escalation to a systemic Cold War or a military

confrontation. In July 2016, the UK's House of Commons
Defence Committee noted, for instance, that 'we cannot hope
for mutual understanding between ourselves and Russia if
we do not have a meaningful dialogue, and under current
conditions of mistrust we run the risk of descent into conflict
that may be preventable through better communication'.[22]

But the argument emphasizing the need for deterrence
has become increasingly dominant. For many in the political and military communities in the Euro-Atlantic area,
deterrence has taken on a 'fundamental importance'. Senior
figures in the US and UK not only suggest that Russia has
become a main priority, but think that 'how to deter Russia
in the twenty-first century has become the most important
question for us'.[23] Then US Secretary of Defense Ashton
Carter stated in June 2016, for instance, that 'we have not
had to prioritise and practice deterrence in Europe for 25
years and while I wish it were otherwise, now we do'.[24]
NATO has also emphasized a shift in priority towards
collective defence and deterrence, and General Scaparrotti,
SACEUR since 2017, has regularly highlighted that deterring Russia is one of his main tasks.[25] This suggests that
the relationship is starting to become a *security paradox*,
'a situation in which two or more actors seeking only to
improve their own security, provoke through their words
or actions an increase in mutual tension resulting in less
security all round'.[26]

The Book's Argument

This book explores these approaches to 'dealing with the
Russians'. With the security dilemma/security challenge/
security paradox at the heart of the argument, this book suggests that while the situation is serious, the problem Russia
poses is being misdiagnosed and the responses, therefore,
poorly framed. The often rather bald dichotomy between
either détente *or* deterring Russia is particularly misleading. Reactive policy is masquerading as strategy – which

is at best only nascent – as the Euro-Atlantic community
is stuck in crisis management mode in its relations with
Russia, and often seems to treat dialogue or deterrence
as ends in themselves, rather than as parts of a coherent
strategic approach.

Chapter 2 reflects on the first level of the security dilemma:
the interpretation of the challenge Russia poses. The chapter
reflects first on how the bilateral relationship is understood,
and the use being made of historical analogies and supposed lessons from history. It then turns to look at how
contemporary Russian challenges are interpreted, particularly
the so-called 'Russian hybrid threat', often known as the
'Gerasimov Doctrine'. Such views and terms have created
an abstract vision of Russia that misdiagnoses the nature
of the challenge, and thus complicate or confuse the dilemma
of response.

Chapter 3 turns to look at the dilemma of response.
It argues that while Euro-Atlantic leaders state that there
will be 'no return to business as usual' or normalization
to pre-Crimea relations, those relations have in fact long
been dysfunctional and problematic. There are few areas
that are truly common interests, and disagreements are
likely to remain entrenched. Consequently, dialogue is
likely to remain a form of managing disagreement, rather
than developing cooperation. The chapter then reflects on
deterrence, sketching out the range of measures currently
being implemented and the difficulties of deterrence, before
considering how deterrence relates to Russia. The chapter
argues that Russian capabilities are evolving and deterrence
therefore needs to be both clearer in its purpose and more
forward-looking.

The final chapter argues that because we have entered
a new era in relations, the categories in which many Euro-
Atlantic policy-makers are thinking and working are no
longer appropriate, and reflects on alternatives and a new
prism for framing where we are. Furthermore, it suggests
that though both dialogue and deterrence are important,
they should be consequences of a broader, coherent approach,

and dealing with the challenges that Moscow presents will
require the development of a clear strategy – and so the
chapter examines steps under way before sketching out
some of the foundations of and variations on what would
be important for such a strategy.

The Difficulties of Empathy: Orthodoxies, Different Chronologies and Superficial Similarities

Given the politicized, often emotional nature of the current
debate about Russia, it is worth framing some caveats about
the scope of the book and its arguments at the outset. First,
the debate about Russia has become highly partisan, as
illustrated perhaps more than anything else (even more
than the military aspects of the tension) by the debate over
'Russia-gate', as Russian interference in US domestic politics
has become known. Some even equated it to Pearl Harbor
and the 9/11 terrorist attacks. The US historian Jackson
Lears put it well, therefore, when he stated that 'with stun-
ning speed a new centrist liberal orthodoxy' has emerged,
a 'secular religion' that excludes dissent. 'Doubters are
perceived as heretics and apologists' for both Trump and
Putin, co-conspirators against democracy,[27] and a new term
has emerged to facilitate this: 'collusion denier'.

This orthodoxy distorts the debates about perception of
the 'Russian threat', serves to turn the debate into a blame
game and masks whether US or NATO actions could themselves be provocative or escalatory – or indeed whether
they are meaningful or effective at all. It also short-circuits
thinking about the central questions. It has led not only to
emphatically delivered but superficial and questionable
assertions about the liberal rules-based order, but to a fixa-
tion on Vladimir Putin and 'Putin's Russia'. Both of these
establish misleading ideas as foundational premises in the
debate. Not only does it – incorrectly – imply that Putin
is some form of omnipotent, omniscient, even prescient
figure, acting decisively on the international stage, but it
isolates Russian activity from any context, and assumes

that Russian 'strategy' is somehow being made in a vacuum in Moscow, and has little to do with either internal developments in Russia or the international context and how the Russian leadership sees their evolution.

For some, therefore, the suggestion that a security dilemma has emerged over the last few years, with its implication that there is reciprocity in the relationship, rather than simply an expansionist threat from Russia, or that Russia itself is engaged in seeking to deter external threats, may be contentious. So let us be clear at the start: Russia poses a major challenge to the Euro-Atlantic community. This challenge is serious and there should be little doubt about it given that Moscow's disagreements with the Euro-Atlantic community, both of values and of policies, are repeatedly made explicit by the Russian authorities themselves. It is on this foundation that the book seeks to explore nuances in the relationship, the nature of the challenge, and the appropriate responses to it. The challenge is based, though, not on an expansive, aggressive Russian plan, but instead on a series of contemporary (if long-running) policy disagreements that are emphasized by different understandings of today's international environment.

A central – if somewhat implicit – point the book makes is that contemporary debates in the Euro-Atlantic community and Russia are starting the history of the relationship from different points in time and thus working effectively in what might be called different time zones. This serves to highlight the range of confusions, as well as disagreements. The starting point for many Euro-Atlantic analyses of Russian activity – and how it should be dealt with – is usually early 2014. Many track back from this point – effectively using history as a search for origins – drawing a direct line of Russian aggression from the war in Georgia, pausing to note Putin's return to the Kremlin in 2012, often asserted as the moment when Russian foreign policy became more aggressive towards the West, and then progressing through to the annexation of Crimea and the war in Ukraine before hypothesizing about what will come

next – usually an anticipated Russian incursion into Moldova
or the Baltic states. Illustrating this, those who have tested
the idea of defending the Baltic states have stated that Putin
'has now attacked neighbouring states three times'. After
Ukraine, they argued, the 'next most likely targets for
attempted Russian coercion are the Baltics ... [T]his story
line is disturbingly familiar.'[28]

As different crises have subsequently struck the relationship, whether interference in domestic affairs, cyber
security or the poisoning of the Skripals, the 'history as
origins' theme has developed – as different episodes such as
the cyber attack on Estonia in 2007 and the 2006 murder
of former Russian security services officer Alexander Litvinenko have been added to it. This poses a complex knot
of 'past as present', one that shapes – but also renders
rigid – an orthodox but partial view of Russia and the set
of problems it poses.

The Russian leadership sees a very different chronology.
Moscow's timeline for its view of the Euro-Atlantic community usually begins in the 1990s, most obviously with
the alleged promise to not enlarge NATO and then with
NATO's campaign against Serbia in 1999. But an important
point of departure in Russian thinking is 2002–4, when
the US withdrew from the Anti-Ballistic Missile (ABM)
Treaty and invaded Iraq in a pre-emptive campaign that it
asserted was defensive. Furthermore, Moscow suffered a
series of setbacks in 2004, including the Orange Revolution
in Ukraine and a series of serious terrorist attacks. The
Russian leadership asserts Western involvement through
support for local actors, whether they be Ukrainian political groups or Chechen terrorists. This Russian version of
history – partially (at best) remembered by most contemporary Western policy-makers and observers – underpins
Russian policy-making, and is the context in which subsequent milestones such as Putin's speech at the Munich
Security Conference in 2007, and Russia's responses to the
so-called 'Arab Spring' beginning in 2011, and to the Euro-
Maidan protests in Ukraine in 2013–14, should be seen.

Equally, there is a striking superficial similarity in the discussions about the relationship in the Euro-Atlantic community and in Russia – there is much discussion, for instance, of a new Cold War.[29] But this debate is an almost direct inversion of that familiar to the Euro-Atlantic community. If observers and officials in the Euro-Atlantic community assert that Russia has invented and been waging 'hybrid warfare', the Russian debate is about how the West invented it and has been waging it against Russia. If the Euro-Atlantic community criticizes Russia for its actions in Syria, such as the bombing of Aleppo, Moscow points to Western attacks on Raqqa and Mosul. If the Euro-Atlantic community points to how the Russian leadership uses cyber attacks and a disinformation or propaganda campaign against the West, this is mirrored in the Russian discussion about how Russia is under constant cyber attack and faces an intensive information war.[30] When the Euro-Atlantic community focuses on cyber attacks on Estonia in 2007, Moscow points to such attacks on Iran in 2015. And if the Euro-Atlantic discussion is focused on how Moscow interferes in its domestic politics, the Russian leadership has long argued that the US (among other Western states) interferes in Russian domestic politics.[31] Indeed, the Russian leadership sees a highly competitive international environment, and a potentially existential threat being posed to it by the US-led Euro-Atlantic community. Much of what the Russian leadership is attempting to implement is its own form of deterrence – primarily deterrence against perceived threats posed by a US-led West.

This emphasizes the need to attempt empathy, the attempt to put oneself in another's shoes. Empathy is not synonymous with sympathy: to recognize that Moscow sees the world differently – and attempting to understand that difference – does not mean accepting its veracity, or urging compromise with it. And again, none of this is to deny that there are serious policy disagreements between the Euro-Atlantic community and Russia, or Moscow's role in contributing to the rapid deterioration of relations. Indeed, quite the opposite: it is to suggest that as a result of these disconnections, these disagreements are becoming more intense. Dealing with them is at the heart of the matter.

Second, the primary point of focus in the book is the Euro-Atlantic community's views of and policy towards Russia, with particular emphasis on relations between Russia and NATO, the EU, the UK and the US. This is not an assertion that there is widespread consensus across NATO and the EU, let alone all of their member states, or even in London or Washington – in the latter, for instance, there are evident gaps between the President and large parts of the body politic and US bureaucracy. Policy and the debate about Russia are not undifferentiated: as discussed throughout the book, there are ongoing and often quite vigorous debates over a number of questions. It is instead to illuminate the official documents and statements about Russia and policies towards it, as well as the nature of discussion about Russia under way in the public policy communities and the mainstream media.

And while the book addresses the broader Euro-Atlantic relationship with Russia, within that it illuminates the UK's relationship with Russia. If the US–Russia, NATO–Russia and EU–Russia relationships are already widely debated in research and media alike, UK–Russia relations remain much less thoroughly examined. The UK–Russia relationship has its own specific characteristics: though there are important examples of cooperation, there is a pronounced element of rivalry in the relationship, and the debate in respective national medias is often vitriolic. Russian politicians and observers have accused the UK of being Russia's 'official enemy', and being the conspiratorial culprit in many unhappy Russian episodes, from the murder of Alexander Griboedov in Tehran in 1829 to the 'provocation' of perestroika. Their British counterparts reciprocate in kind; Bernard Shaw's statement in 1914 that Russia 'is the enemy of every liberty we boast of' remains a widely held view in British political circles, and the Committee of State Security (KGB) and Russian agents feature prominently in contemporary British conspiracy theories.[32]

Shedding light on London's view of and relationship with Russia is important. It illuminates the point that UK–Russia relations are closely entwined with, and in many ways mirror, the wider Euro-Atlantic's relationship with Russia, reflecting its successes, failures, frustrations and problems. The UK has played a prominent, if at times ambiguous, role in the Euro-Atlantic community's response to Russia since 2014, hosting NATO's Wales summit and contributing to NATO's enhanced Forward Presence (eFP). This became more evident still with the events in Salisbury in March 2018 and in Syria that put the UK and Russia on a more confrontational course. Moreover, the vote to leave the EU has prompted London to attempt both to shape a 'Global Britain' horizon, and, as British officials repeatedly emphasize, to seek to defend the liberal international rules-based order – both of which are likely to bring the UK into ever more contact and competition with Russia. The UK–Russia angle is brought out more prominently, therefore, in the final chapter, which considers the need for a strategy to deal with Russia. Not only is this harmonious with the broader trajectory of Euro-Atlantic–Russia relations, but as London attempts to formulate a Russia strategy, some of the main features (and difficulties) of so doing can offer a model and some lessons that are applicable to other Euro-Atlantic states as they too begin to do so.

Finally, in exploring the question of 'dealing with the Russians', the book offers an argument about relations particularly with the Russian state and leadership, often using the shorthand of 'Russia' or 'Moscow' (rather than the wider Russian population), interpreting the nature of the problem and sketching out foundation pillars of a strategy. A core part of this is that relations with Russia have entered a new era, and the book tries to think in these bigger terms. In so doing, it touches on a wide range of subjects and raises numerous issues and questions, some of which, though they are relevant and important, are not explored in depth. Moscow's positions on some Western policies and the evolution of Russian capabilities and deterrence form an important part of the book's scope, for example. But the book does not seek to address Russian foreign and security policy writ large, in terms of either Moscow's policy priorities, or wider questions such as Russian diplomacy (and coalition building) in the Middle East or Russia's relations with China.

Equally, this is not a book about some of the currently prominent specific questions, such as the war in Ukraine or US–Russia relations and 'Russia-gate'. Again, these important issues feature at different points throughout. But not only are they already widely discussed elsewhere, they are parts of a larger problem, in terms of both definition and response, and the book treats them in that wider context. While the book sketches out a working definition of deterrence, it does not dwell on either the theory of nuclear deterrence, or specific technical questions such as cyber deterrence and deterrence in space.[33]

It seems that relations are – yet again – at a difficult moment. There are long-running and deeply entrenched disagreements which are both well known and unlikely to be resolved in the short term, and yet simultaneously developments are fast moving, with new crisis coming upon crisis. This book focuses on illuminating the broader debate about relations with Russia, and the evolution in relations from one era to the next. It is time to move beyond seeing specific developments as individual 'difficult moments' or 'crises', in the sense of the turning point of an illness, when an important change takes place, suggesting either recovery or death, and to understand them more as *paroxysms*, sudden but recurring intensifications in a pattern of the normalization of the symptoms. A structural state of relations has taken shape since the early 2000s, one that cannot easily or quickly be overcome. To deal effectively with this will require the retirement of the worn-out and out-of-date repetitions, and the tired clichés and template phrases that currently dominate the public policy lexicon about Russia, that purport to offer ready-made solutions. These should be replaced with fresh thinking. The second step is to shape an active, coherent and well-resourced strategy for dealing with Russia over the next decade.

2
(Mis)interpreting the Russian Threat

The dilemma of interpretation is at the heart of the overall question of dealing with the Russians. For many, as outlined in the introduction, it is already resolved: Russia is seen as aggressive and to pose a threat to international order, a revisionist power that, according to the new US National Security Strategy, uses 'technology, propaganda and coercion to shape a world antithetical to our interests and values'. Russia is seen as a challenge to American power, influence and interests, and to be attempting to 'erode US security and prosperity'.[1]

This represents a quick and significant shift in perspective. Few, if any, would have suggested in 2013 that Russia was a near-peer or peer competitor to the Euro-Atlantic world, for instance, particularly in terms of military and defence. Indeed, the prevailing view was represented by the #Sochiproblems campaign documenting the failures and problems of the 2014 Winter Olympics, seen to be illustrative of Russian weakness and incompetence. The shock of the annexation of Crimea just weeks later, and the sudden concerns that Russia challenged the entire Euro-Atlantic security edifice, meant that in the space of a couple of years Russia has turned from being 'merely' a regional power, one acting out of weakness, as then President Obama put it, to one that has a global reach, and to one of such influence that it has become the culprit of choice for many, if not most, of the problems that the Euro-Atlantic community faces, one that can wield a wide range of tools, from energy and information to the military to achieve its policy aims.

Yet much of the discussion about Russia misdiagnoses the nature of the challenge, depicting an abstract, essentialist, unchanging version of Russia, through snapshots and simplified analogies and sound bites. Based on the foundation of a loss of self-confidence in the Euro-Atlantic policy community, the problem of interpretation can be found at two levels: how the bilateral relationship is understood, and how Russian activities more specifically are interpreted. This chapter looks at each in turn.

Returning to Cold War Relations?

Odd Arne Westad, a prominent historian of the Cold War, suggested in 2018 that 'for about four years now, since Russia's occupation of Crimea and China's launch of the Belt and Road initiative, there has been much speculation about whether another Cold War between East and West is coming'.[2] Discussion of a 'new Cold War', a 'return to Cold War' or a 'Cold War II (or 2.0)' between Russia and the West is pervasive, with each new negative turn in relations being a 'new low' since the end of the Cold War, and 'reminiscent' of the Cold War. Haass also reflected the views of many when he stated that we 'unexpectedly find ourselves in a second Cold War, both different and familiar'. The 'lion's share of responsibility' for this, he argued, is 'Russia's, and above all Vladimir Putin's', since the Russian President 'viewed the US dominated world order as a threat to his rule and to what he regarded as his country's rightful place in the world'.[3]

With the publication of new US National Security and Defense Strategies in late 2017 and early 2018, *Time* magazine suggested that the Trump administration 'harkens back to the Cold War era', while others asserted that Putin wanted to 'go back to the good old days' and is 'back to fighting the Cold War, even if we in the West are not'.[4] In spring 2018, as the United Nations (UN) Secretary General Antonio Guterres stated that the 'Cold War was back with a vengeance',[5] *Foreign Affairs* journal carried the point that 'so concerned have Westerners grown with [Putin's] political meddling, regional aggression and general efforts to play international spoiler that many of them contend we are entering a new Cold War. Are we?' To answer this, it published the anthology *A New Cold War? Russia and the United States, Then and Now*, republishing many prominent articles by leading thinkers and practitioners, sewing together articles from George Kennan's 1947 piece 'The Sources of Soviet Conduct' and the early 1950s through to contemporary times.[6] *National Interest* followed suit, with an edition entitled 'A New Cold War', including articles asserting that 'Cold War II' is a rematch among the same teams, the need for containment, and reflecting on what Kennan would make of it all.

There are understandable reasons for asserting that the current situation is a 'return to Cold War': it is a convenient way of indicating that there is a sense of systemic disagreement between the US and Russia. Each side frames the standoff in unforgiving terms, and seeks to pin the blame entirely on the other for the emergence of the more adversarial relationship. There is also a paucity of reasoned dialogue or introspection, and a number of proxy conflicts have emerged, most obviously in Ukraine and Syria.[7] But this is the first indication that the dilemma of interpretation is well on the way to being resolved, considerably simplifying the range of responses. Russia can easily be framed as a challenge already (successfully) faced in the past. This poses serious problems for understanding Russia today and how to deal with it. Four can be noted here.

New Cold War Groundhog Day

First, the 'return to Cold War' variations have become little more than stock or 'filler' phrasing, with any meaning – beyond that the Euro-Atlantic community and Russia have a bad relationship – worn out by a repetitive overuse that serves to obscure how relations have evolved and deteriorated over the course of ten to fifteen years and why. It offers a 'Groundhog Day' effect: the debate seems stuck in a regularly recurring and re-setting time loop: though without there appearing to be any learning or progress with the succession of loops. (The usual way for the protagonist to escape a time loop is acquiring knowledge, using retained memories to progress and eventually exit the loop. The time loop is thus a problem-solving process, and the narrative becomes akin to an interactive puzzle. This is lacking from most discussion of Euro-Atlantic relations with Russia.)[8]

Though Westad suggests that speculation about a new Cold War has been under way since 2014, it has actually haunted the debate about relations since the early 1990s, and became a central feature of the Euro-Atlantic debate about Russia from the mid-2000s. Quotes from some of Putin's speeches are used to lend emphasis – particularly one he made in 2005 in which he referred to the collapse of the Union of Soviet Socialist Republics (USSR) as being the greatest geopolitical catastrophe of the twentieth century, and another in Munich in February 2007, a speech heralded by many to be a declaration of a 'new Cold War'.[9] Since then, versions on the theme of a 'return to Cold War' or 'Cold War déjà vu', or 'Cold War 2.0' – all signifying a supposed 'return to the old ways' of European security – have reappeared more or less yearly with every new deterioration in relations, only accelerating with the outbreak of war in Ukraine in 2014.[10]

In the mid-2000s, the 'return to Cold War' argument generated a number of convincing refutations. Not only were conditions different to the original Cold War, but the scale and scope of the dissonance between the Euro Atlantic community and Russia were not the same: there were fundamental conflicts neither of interest nor of ideology, as there had been throughout the Cold War. A self-sustaining polemic thus took shape, one that became increasingly acrimonious with the outbreak of war in Ukraine – often depicted as being between 'Cold Warriors' and 'Putin apologists'. Through constant repetition, both sides of the argument have become automatic, even dogmatic, even as the situation evolved.

Ideology, for instance, is becoming a more explicit feature of the relationship, especially since 2016. If differences in *values* were obvious in the mid-to-late 2000s, there was no sense of ideological confrontation. The influence of the 'End of History' arguments in the early 1990s – simply put as the disappearance of ideological challenges to liberal democracy – combined with the widespread view that Russia would 'return to the Western family of nations' through a process of domestic transition to democracy and international partnership with the West, meant that ideological confrontation was not part of the post-Cold War calculus. (Though it is worth noting that while the 'End of History' argument suggested that there was no ideological confrontation, this meant that *counterpart ideologies* had disappeared, while values began to replace interests in US foreign policy priorities.)[11]

But when Biden urges citizens to mobilize against the threat posed by the 'Russian government brazenly assaulting the foundations of Western democracy around the world',[12] can this still be said to be the case? This is of a different order to the critique of Russia's failure to move in the 'right direction' (towards democracy and partnership with the Euro-Atlantic community), and even the democratic roll-back that characterized much of the 2000s. Though Biden correctly suggests that the Kremlin 'offers no clear ideology of its own', this has the sense, if not yet the structure, of a stronger ideological element, at least on the part of elements of the Euro-Atlantic community.

Furthermore, although there are numerous longer-term policy disagreements, the scale and geographical scope of these disagreements have grown considerably, even since 2014, and seem likely to continue to do so. The dissonance of interests has developed beyond the regional level, where it escalated to a severe point in Ukraine, to a much wider, even global scale. Russia's presence – and Moscow's policy disagreements with the Euro-Atlantic community – is to be felt in Syria for instance, but also in the Arctic, Central Asia, North Africa and beyond. The limits of Russian capabilities in the 2010s mean that this wider competition has not been as structural as it was during the second half of the twentieth century, but again the sense was illustrated when Moscow deployed a flotilla of warships to the north of Australia during the G20 in November 2014.[13]

Finally, relations have become so bad since 2016 that many on both sides have observed that they are *worse* and more dangerous than during the Cold War. Some suggest that the situation is more dangerous than the Cold War because there is no 'focus on a strategic relationship between Moscow and Washington'.[14] Others observe that during the Cold War there were many mechanisms for confidence building and crisis response. These have been lost, and there are too few structural safety valves.

The many variations on the 'Cold War' theme, both those arguing for and those arguing against it, ignore or obscure this evolution and the causes of the significant deterioration over the last decade, and even bury it under a cloak of dogmatism about Putin's supposed attempts to resurrect the USSR, or that Moscow is pursuing a renewed expansionist drive. But there are other problems with the 'return to Cold War' argument.

Analogies and the Problems of 20/60 Hindsight

The second problem is the use of the Cold War as an analogical tool to understand the nature of the relationship and what responses are appropriate. Rather than offering supposed benefits of hindsight, however, analogical use of history often introduces a form of intellectual short-sightedness, a myopic focus on arbitrarily chosen events or dates – effectively a form of 20/60 vision. The difficulties of this are well known. In 1973, the US historian of international affairs Ernest May wrote that history is often used badly in international politics: in resorting to analogy, officials and observers tend to seize on the first that comes to mind, without searching more broadly, analysing the case to test its appropriateness or asking in which ways it is misleading.[15] There is a complex of reasons why this is so with the Cold War analogies.

Many questions of the Cold War remain unresolved, and the overall picture remains fragmentary – there are many myths about it, and choosing which lessons to draw is not easy.[16] Nevertheless, if it is true, as the Professor of War Studies Lawrence Freedman suggested in 2010, that 'as the years pass, the Cold War increasingly appears as an undifferentiated chunk of history stretching across time and space', a convenient but misleading label for a time that has taken on an 'institutionalised, ritualised quality that rarely seems to have posed any danger of giving way to the chaos and catastrophe of total war',[17] the Cold War presents a curiously moving target for analogies. This is partly because conditions evolved substantially throughout the Cold War, not just through specific crises or periods of détente, but because the perceived balance of power was in constant flux and there was significant social, economic, political and technical change throughout the fifty or so years of the Cold War era. Thus even the meanings of terms used, such as deterrence and containment, evolved during the Cold War.

This dynamic but complex picture is complicated still further by the evolution in understanding of the Cold War in the short post-Cold War era – from understandable relief and euphoria in the early 1990s, to a more reflective and analytical approach during the 2000s, to a more emotionally charged period since 2014. This is important because the questions posed of the Cold War period change with this evolution: the analogies and evidence used are shaped by the questions of the present, and as the questions change, what is prioritized, what is selected to be remembered and what is forgotten – the 'answers' to what the Cold War 'meant' – have quickly evolved. As the historian Herbert Butterfield noted, without self-discipline, the prejudices of the day are projected onto the past, confirming 'prevailing fallacies and ratifying the favourite errors of the day, even magnifying the prejudices of each stage of history by projecting them back on the canvas of all the centuries'.[18]

What the Cold War 'meant' in 2010, therefore, is rather different to what it 'meant' in 2015 and 2018. It seems not long ago that officials, politicians and observers looked back on the Cold War as a time of calm, even as a time of comparative simplicity. Retired officials and observers alike have noted that during the wars in Iraq and Afghanistan and the war on terror, people wistfully looked back to the Cold War as a time when at least they knew who the enemy was. As Freedman pointed out in 2010, it had become 'common to talk of the reassuring rationality and predictability of the old Soviet adversary, with unfavourable comparisons to Washington's current enemies'.[19] This does not sit well alongside current notions of Russian unpredictability.

This leads to another problem: thinking in terms of Cold War analogy encourages too strong a sense of familiarity. As Kofman has pointed out, it is 'tempting for US Cold Warriors simply to cross out "Soviet Union", write in "Russia" and look to set up the same Air-Land Battle as they played out on many a hex square table top exercise in the 1980s'. There is even a 'gap' to fight over: instead of the Cold War's 'Fulda Gap', today there is the 'Suwalki Gap'.[20]

And, indeed, there is often a sense that by thinking about the challenges that contemporary Russia poses in the light of the Cold War, decisions can be made with the minimum of fresh analysis. Many of the responses bear the hallmarks of this – much of the language and terminology used in today's discussion about Russia recalls the Cold War, from the frequent citation of Winston Churchill and George Kennan, to the talk of Putin's intentions to restore the Soviet Union or 'take Russia back to the Soviet era', and of the need 'to contain' Russia, the deployment of 'trip-wire' forces to Eastern Europe as part of NATO's eFP (it is to be hoped that these in due course do not become 'flexible response' forces),[21] and concerns about an arms race, with all its emotional baggage of nuclear weapons, mutually assured destruction and Armageddon.

This permits assumptions today about the Cold War that are not necessarily true, particularly running the risk of being taken in by legends of success during that time. But the West did not always well understand Soviet military thinking and capability: for instance, there was much mis-understanding of how the Soviets would conduct a campaign against NATO. Similarly, myths tend to dominate thinking. As the US academic Thomas Mahnken has noted, the myth of containment is often invoked: a simplified, idealized representation of a family of strategies that successive US administrations had pursued over decades. But it has become, he notes, an 'empty vessel to be filled with whatever scholars and policy-makers desire or fear', and it has been used since the end of the Cold War in virtually every contem-porary challenge, including Iran, China and Al Qaeda. It is thus a 'surrogate for thinking through US aims, perform-ing assessment and developing a strategy'.[22]

The Problems of Déjà Vu in the New Era

Such an approach is dangerous. The world has changed beyond recognition since the Cold War era. Politics, society and culture have all evolved substantially, including the role of the media, and there are many more influential actors in both domestic and international politics. The bipolar confrontation is no longer the centrepiece of inter-national affairs: the rise of China, instability in the Middle East and problems such as terrorism, migration and climate change all alter the strategic horizon. These changes are compounded by different approaches to security in the Euro-Atlantic community. Societies were not just demobilized after the Cold War but became demilitarized – with a concomitant different approach to defence spending as part of electoral campaigns. Thinking also evolved from collective defence to collective security, through the prisms of the post-Cold War peace dividend, the 9/11 terrorist attacks and the wars in Iraq and Afghanistan. It is not possible simply to 'revert' to a Cold War approach.

This is partly because the range and scale of capabilities available to Western leaders, both material and intellectual, are very different. With the change in strategic focus in the 1990s and 2000s, there has been a loss of practical, technical knowledge across the Euro-Atlantic community, whether about Russian tactics and doctrine or in recognition of equipment, and a loss of much expertise, for instance in massed artillery and ordnance clearing. During the Cold War, some two thirds of the US intelligence budget was focused on the USSR, most of that on battle order data. And at its height, there were 400,000 US soldiers assigned to Europe and 6,000 battle tanks. The post-Cold War period saw a significant reduction: in 2013, the last US main battle tank left Europe, and only 35,000 soldiers remained.

After two decades of reforms, only a very few NATO member states are capable of conducting full spectrum combat operations, and, apart from the US, none can pursue them alone. Senior European officers note that the capability to fight collective manoeuvre warfare has been lost over the last fifteen years. This reflected the significant shift of the Euro-Atlantic community's attention. As the UK's House of Commons Defence Committee stated, for twenty years the UK and other NATO member states focused on terrorism and failed states and counter-insurgency. This entailed focus on precision weapons, small-scale operations, low casualties – a very different kind of war from the Cold War, and a shift that had meant very different force profiles and procurement, training, exercises and logistics. It had meant a transition from thinking and preparing for a collective defence and existential war to expeditionary wars of choice.

And the geography is different. With NATO enlargement, the alliance's strategic horizon is changed. This poses three sets of problems: not only are the deployment distances much longer from main bases in Western Europe, but the infrastructure is less well developed. Second, due to civil restrictions, there are complications moving military materiel around Europe. Third, because of the geography of Eastern Europe, considerations of defence are completely altered: the locations of Belarus, a Russian ally, and particularly Kaliningrad, a heavily fortified Russian exclave, mean that Russian forces encircle NATO member states. As Kofman notes, therefore, 'picking up a Cold War fight, moving it over a few hundred kilometres and putting it down in the Baltics is not the right way to think about it. The world has changed, and there is a need to adjust to the geopolitical landscape of today.'[23]

The Cold War as a Screen Analogy

The fourth main problem with 'return to Cold War' variations is that the Cold War analogy acts as a 'screen analogy' that permits the smuggling in of a rather different question: the rise of 1930s Nazi Germany, the Munich Agreement of 1938, World War II and the implications of Germany's defeat, particularly symbolic reference to the 1945 Yalta conference. This transforms an albeit difficult intellectual effort to learn from history into an emotional sacred tale. Officials and observers explicitly use the Nazi analogy when referring to Vladimir Putin and Russia. Indeed, such comparisons are frequently made: if the UK's Foreign Secretary, Boris Johnson, caused a scandal when he compared the 2018 football World Cup to the Nazi Olympics, he was not the first: US Senator Lindsey Graham had done much the same regarding the 2014 Sochi Winter Olympics. Lithuanian President Dalia Grybauskaite was among those who stated that Putin uses nationality as a pretext to conquer territory with military means much as Stalin and Hitler did, and many, including Hillary Clinton and John Baird, then Canadian Foreign Minister, compared the annexation of Crimea to Hitler's territorial moves prior to World War II. Lieutenant General Stephen Wilson, then commanding general of US Global Air Strike Command, exemplified the common view when he stated that 'some of the actions by Russia recently we haven't seen since the 1930s when whole countries were annexed and borders changed by force'.[24]

There are variations on the Nazi Germany analogy, ranging from reference to the Russian Yunarmiya as an equivalent of the Hitler Youth to how the actions of Russian forces in Aleppo echo those of the Condor Legion's actions in Guernica. But the analogy of the Munich Agreement is most pervasive. If there are those who have suggested that the Minsk II agreement is 'worse than Munich',[25] the UK's then Prime Minister David Cameron is one of many who have referred to not 'repeating the same mistakes' with Russia as had been made appeasing Hitler in Munich in 1938.[26]

The prevalence of the Nazi Germany analogy is an indication of the high emotion in the relationship. It is another indication that the first level of the security dilemma has already been resolved: as Fettweis has vividly stated, 'if there is one iron-clad indicator of the enemy image, it is the comparison of rivals to the Nazis', and Hitler analogies are often rhetorical, used to support policy decisions already made (he added that 'when Nazis haunt decision-makers, folly follows').[27]

But it is also an indicator of how thinking about Russia is stuck in the twentieth century, and of the repetitive, stereotypical nature of thinking about international challenges. The Munich myth is one of the most powerful and influential political myths of the second half of the twentieth century. The former British civil servant turned academic David Chuter put it elegantly when he stated in 1998 that there is 'scarcely a major crisis of this era where its baleful ghost has not peered through the windows of conferences and crisis meetings, and scarcely a foreign and security policy which does not show its influence'.[28]

The use of the Munich myth is important because of the lessons that it supposedly teaches. It is usually invoked to demonstrate the need to stand up to aggression and to avoid appeasing dictators. As Chuter argued, it is didactic, offering an 'orderly schema of error and punishment, a cause-and-effect relationship so obvious as to be universally accepted': if something different had been done in the 1930s, then the consequences would have been different and tragedy avoided. This shares many characteristics of myth-making in international affairs, and three stand out here.

First, it rests on a 'sacred text' (all myths, Chuter noted, have a sacred text) – in this case, Hitler's book *Mein Kampf*, which was widely held to have been a blueprint for the well-thought-out, progressive scheme which Hitler later implemented in detail. Second, it is built on the assumption that history can be understood largely to repeat itself, that Munich-type situations recur and, having learnt what to do, leaders can thus act in a more informed way to avoid repetition of a disaster. Third, if Munich acts as a surrogate for all the perceived inaction and mistakes of the 1930s, it offers a cartoon-like simplicity, reducing all the complexity of the situation to black and white to shape a simple pattern of aggressor, victim and the consequences that will follow if intervention is not performed. It becomes an idealistic, humanitarian, persuasive tool to drive arguments for policy decisions.

But the Cold War and 1930s Nazi Germany analogies have become implicitly blended to offer a compound analogy. Many Cold War policies were based on the belief that Stalin was Hitler's successor. Jeffrey Record, Professor of Strategy at the US Air War College, for example, notes that Munich conditioned the thinking of every Cold War US presidential administration.[29] And much of the basis of the Cold War era strategies of containment and deterrence was founded on understandings of the 1930s: Western fears of Soviet aggressive intent drew on previous experiences, particularly the events leading up to World War II. The Munich Syndrome loomed large, Beatrice Heuser, a historian and Professor of International Relations, has suggested, as an 'ignominious attempt to appease Hitler' which had not succeeded – and therefore the fear of any gesture implying appeasement was present in dealings with Stalin. She cites George Kennan's recollection of the climate of thought at the outset of the Korean war:

> It was hard to get the Pentagon to desist from seeing in Stalin another Hitler and fighting the last war all over again in its plans for the next one ... our military – and to some extent our political – planners ... could not free themselves from the image of Hitler and his timetables. They viewed the Soviet leaders as absorbed with something called the 'grand design' – a design for the early destruction of American power and for world conquest.[30]

In blurring the differences between the presumed, familiar and known, these myths serve to cut short arguments about policy responses to Russia. They remove the value of history, partly because the analogy is pulled out of the context of its history: as Chuter pointed out, the Munich analogy has become completely detached from the circumstances of 1938, and disregards the perceptions and limitations politicians faced at the time.[31] These analogies also misrepresent the nature of the problem, asserting that the challenge that Russia poses – and the one that has to be deterred – is an essentialist one of Russian expansionism, one that echoes the Hitlerite model of a well-thought-out scheme, progressive in nature and the product of rational cost–benefit analysis, and that if the Russian leadership is confronted with a higher price than they are willing to pay, then Moscow will back down.

Learning from History?

This is not to say that history is unimportant, or that nothing can be learnt from the Cold War era. But learning from the

Cold War era is achieved through neither endless repeti-tive lists of similarities or dissimilarities to the Cold War, nor the reiteration of analogies and myths, which only serves to render thinking dogmatic. Nor do the shibboleths of the Cold War provide adequate material for learning lessons in completely different circumstances. This is history without History.

Since the Nazi Germany analogy is so prevalent in the debate, it is worth remembering French historian Marc Bloch's analysis of France's defeat in 1940. He stated that the failure was 'due to a lack of imagination and a tendency to take refuge from the urgency of fact in abstractions'. Many mistakes were made, he argued, including how the memories of glories of the previous war had been baked into the marrow of the bones of the French leadership, with the result that 'thinking was done in terms of yesterday or the day before' and a 'susceptibility to ready-made for-mulae'. 'The enemy, because we had never learned enough about him, rarely did what we expected him to ... [and] refused to play the game according to staff college rules', Bloch continued. The policy pursued after 1918, he stated, was based on a picture of Europe which no longer existed: leaders were more afraid of the Hohenzollerns than of Adolf Hitler, who posed a completely different challenge, and were 'mainly concerned to renew in 1940 the condi-tions of the war they had waged in 1914–18'.[32] And as the British thinker Basil Liddell Hart stated, 'the most danger-ous delusions are those that arise from the sentimental misinterpretation of history or its deliberate distortion ... such treatment of war hinders necessary changes to meet changing conditions. It conceals faults that might otherwise be remedied.'[33]

History and historiography can help to understand current challenges. Above and beyond finding continuity or sup-posed repetitive patterns, history is about understanding *change and novelty*, cause and effect. History does not repeat itself. As Bloch argued, no two events are alike, because the conditions from which they spring are never identical, and the number of possible combinations is almost infinite. The educative value of history is not therefore that what happened yesterday will necessarily happen tomorrow, or that the past will go on reproducing itself. Instead, through examining how and why yesterday differed from the day before, one can reflect on how tomorrow will differ from yesterday. In this way, he pointed out that 'the historian is well aware that no two successive wars are ever the same war, because in the period between them, a number of modifications have occurred in the social structures of the countries concerned, in the progress of technical skill and in the minds of men'.[34]

In terms more akin to historiography, reflecting on Cold War era thinking can be revealing – and relevant to today – particularly how Cold War era officials and observers alike reflected on their work. This is usually missing from the current new Cold War debate, but it raises three essential points. First, the 'principal fault' in assessing the adversary was the 'inability to empathize with the other side and to visualize its interests in other than adversarial terms' – and those whose assessments conflicted with orthodoxy were given short shrift. Thus, there was 'never adequate recognition' in US assessments, Raymond Garthoff argued, of the need to weigh Soviet threat assessments and concerns over US military buildup activities, alliance building and global basing. Instead, assessments suffered from mirror-imaging and related misjudgement of Soviet strategic priorities.

The second problem was the difficulty of grasping that the Soviet Union not only understood security in very different ways, but suffered similar problems trying to understand the West: as one noted, the Soviets were not always able to understand NATO documents – only the NATO-ese could fully understand NATO-speak. As Brent Scowcroft noted, one lesson stands out above all others: neither side was infallible in the judgements made about the adversary. Mirror-imaging and unfounded assumptions were almost always seriously misleading and at times dangerous.

The third problem was the difficulty of assessing Soviet capabilities – and the numerous cases of underestimation and overestimation, as reflected in the bomber and missile gap disputes, and failure to notice Russian weakness alongside underestimations of Western strength.[35] Many of these problems remain today, and provide the real basis for learning from the Cold War era.

The Abstraction of the Russian Threat

The second broad problem of interpreting Russia is at the more specific level of Russian activity and capabilities. Here again, the difficulty is in conceptualization of the problem, the application of buzzwords and abstract labels to define it – once more we encounter contemporary versions of Bloch's ready-made formula and abstractions. Though these labels serve to give a new, contemporary feel to the debate about Russia, they are often couched in the wider 'return to Cold War' context.[36]

Anti-Access/Area Denial – 'A2/AD'

One feature of the discussion about Euro-Atlantic security is Russia's Anti-Access/Area Denial (A2/AD), a term which is considered to capture the security and political challenge posed by Moscow's military investments along NATO's frontiers. As one observer has put it, 'over the past few years, Russia has deployed sophisticated anti-air and anti-ship defences, bombers and missiles at key locations' to deny enemy access to these regions. This 'calls into question the Alliance's ability to defend the three Baltic states and Poland in case of hostilities with Russia'.[37] Others have suggested that Russia has altered the security balance in the Black Sea, Eastern Mediterranean and Middle East by establishing large A2/AD exclusion zones or 'bubbles', 'challenging NATO's position', and that not only has Russia's power projection capability in these regions extended, but there is an 'A2/AD arms race'.

In so doing, A2/AD has 'crossed the buzzword threshold', becoming a part of NATO jargon and the strategic debate about capabilities and war-fighting. Moscow's A2/AD capabilities 'seem to challenge NATO's erstwhile assumption that Moscow could be deterred by a readiness-only approach that ensured allied troops would be in a position to move swiftly' from North America to Eastern Europe.[38]

And to be sure, Russia has developed and deployed powerful and long-range air defence and anti-ship capabilities. But as one officer has pointed out, A2/AD has become a tool to 'manage the confusion and surprise' that Russia's actions have caused in the West. The discussion about A2/AD in the Euro-Atlantic community, he argues, needs to be seen in the context of the hollowing out of many European forces over the last twenty years, and over-focus on multinational expeditionary campaigns in the name of stability and counter-insurgency. 'Having given up many of the high-end war-fighting skills and capabilities', and faced with the Russia question, Western states 'need something that can explain away the conceptual surprise and associated challenge that Russia's actions have caused' and 'come to terms with Russia's confrontational actions, which have been contradictory to the post-Cold War era Western outlook to international politics and strategic affairs'.[39]

As he notes, however, there are problems with the term 'A2/AD' and its application to Russia. The term has empowered Russia: with sensational headlines about new Russian destructive capabilities that can strike deep into NATO, it becomes a loud hailer for Moscow to communicate its discontent about Western actions, causing a frenzy each time it even declares its intent to deploy such capabilities, regardless of whether it does or not. Moreover, by focusing on these Russian capabilities and their ranges, it downplays or ignores the many ways in which they can be neutralized, and the many counter-measures available. Raitasalo rightly argues, therefore, that 'focusing solely on the technical and/or tactical aspects of [the] adversary's military systems may make good headlines, but it does not by itself facilitate the formulation of sound strategy'. Indeed, 'much of the Western A2/AD narrative is located on the military-technical or tactical levels, bypassing the operational, military strategic and grand strategic level thinking and logics'.[40]

This leads to a second set of problems that relate to what A2/AD is supposed to mean. Often presented as something new, especially in Northern Europe, the A2/AD discussion focuses on modern capabilities. But while the specific capabilities may be new, the idea of seeking to deny access to an opponent of course has a long history in warfare,[41] including in Northern Europe. Equally, the bracket of A2/AD, and what Moscow supposedly intends to do with the capabilities that are included under it, has become so inclusive and broad that it loses useful definitional clarity.

Perhaps most importantly, however, while it fits logically into Western, particularly US, military thinking and doctrine, it is just that – a Western approach to understanding a threat that is imposed on Russia through over-focus on technical capabilities laced together with a strong dose of ethnocentrism. Interestingly, the use of the term 'A2/AD' is not restricted to Russia: it is also often used in relation to China – and this serves to emphasize both the limitation of its explanatory value and the dangers in such an approach.

US strategists often refer to Chinese military modernization and capabilities in terms of A2/AD, as an attempt to slow the deployment of forces or to disrupt the ability to conduct operations within a theatre – the emphasis is thus on understanding Chinese military thinking through the question of counter-intervention. Sinologists note, however, that Chinese military writing does not use the term 'A2/AD', except to refer to the US concept, and rarely if ever mentions the concept of counter-intervention. The Chinese military does not use the term A2/AD to describe its own strategy.

The use of the term therefore sustains mirror-imaging, since Chinese military modernization is cast in terms familiar to US defence planners, even though Chinese strategic planners 'display a fundamentally different strategic perspective from the way it is cast in US analysis'. The focus on Chinese A2/AD 'neglects important shifts in structure of the Chinese navy, [and] reduces the objective of Chinese military modernization to one primary mission, thereby overlooking the much broader range of goals that motivate Chinese defence policy'.[42] A2/AD thus compartmentalizes Chinese strategic thinking within a framework that does not reflect the more holistic Chinese approach.[43]

Second, in seeking to ensure that the US retained unmatched conventional military superiority across all domains (air, sea, land, space and cyberspace) and preserved the ability to mass forces and enter a combat zone decisively, US planners developed Air-Sea Battle, a concept that seeks to integrate the capabilities of air and naval forces to ensure US freedom of action (the doctrine became official in 2010 and in 2015 was renamed Joint Concept for Access and Maneuver in the Global Commons). The result is that certain Chinese capabilities are evolving to counter Air-Sea Battle on the one hand, and on the other, there is a concern among some in the US that Air-Sea Battle could be misunderstood in China as posing a risk of strikes on the mainland and thus risking escalation. Thus Sinologists suggest that not only does A2/AD not exist in Chinese thinking, but it is creating a security dilemma between the US and China.[44]

These points are pertinent when A2/AD is applied to Russia. Like China, Russia has no new concept or doctrine that would correspond to Western understandings of A2/AD. Indeed, even though Russian military thinkers and planners may think in terms of Western interventionism, and while they may have technical capabilities that fit it, A2/AD is a concept that is foreign to them.[45] Thinking in these terms imposes a Western operational thought process onto the Russian one, creating a mirror image. It also illuminates just one part of the wider Russian security horizon, giving a misleading picture of how Russian operations would take shape if hostilities erupted, because it does not consider what else would be going on at the same time. And by removing it from the context of Russian military thinking, it can too easily obscure or exclude consideration of the doubts and difficulties that the Russian military leadership faces, not least the defence of the exclave Kaliningrad and its encirclement by NATO states.

By rendering Russian security thinking in abstract Western conceptual terms, therefore, the sense of Russian threat can be magnified (diminishing the sense that this has defensive features), while simultaneously the likelihood of being surprised by actual Russian activity is increased. While Russia has advanced capabilities in this field, focusing on A2/AD means that thinking about Russia remains at the tactical and technical level, and concentrated on an understanding of (some) capabilities, not how and in what ways they may be used and to what ends. This term should be quickly and finally retired from the discussion about Russia.

'Russian Hybrid Warfare' and 'the Gerasimov Doctrine'

Yet more prominent, though, has been the emergence of another buzzword – 'Russian hybrid war' – which began in 2014 in the wake of Russia's annexation of Crimea. This – again – had the feel of a reaction to unwelcome surprise. In their haste to understand what was happening, observers and officials interpreted Russian activity by revisiting some of Putin's most often-cited speeches and embellishing them with reference to assorted other sources to suggest that the Russian leadership had developed a new way of achieving its goals while avoiding direct armed confrontation with the militarily superior West.[46]

Overwhelmingly the most influential of these latter sources was an article published under the name of Chief of the Russian General Staff Valery Gerasimov in the Russian newspaper *Voenno-Promyshlenni Kurier* (*VPK*) in early 2013. The article has become something of a sacred text that underpins a myth: relying heavily on this one source – usually only on translated snippets of it at second or third hand – many Euro-Atlantic commentators and officials suggested that Gerasimov had set out the contours of a new form of Russian warfare that had been deployed in Crimea and Ukraine, reflected in what became known as 'Russian hybrid warfare' or, alternatively, the 'Gerasimov Doctrine'.

This terminology has enjoyed a continuing currency in political, official and media circles. In a widely circulated paper, for instance, the Estonian Foreign Intelligence Service suggested that 'under the Gerasimov Doctrine, the Russian armed forces wage a constant information war'. And US Senator Mark Warner similarly suggested that Gerasimov 'outlined a new security doctrine' for the Kremlin that emphasized 'non-military means', in which hacking, cyber attacks, information warfare and propaganda were the weapons of choice, painting a 'vivid picture of a fight in the shadows – a type of "hybrid warfare"'.[47]

This supposedly new form of war was seen to confer numerous advantages on Moscow: since Russia could not hope to win a conventional war with the West, it had to challenge it in other ways. These include economic manipulation, an extensive and powerful disinformation and propaganda campaign, the fostering of civil disobedience and even insurrection and the use of well-supplied paramilitaries. In sum, 'Russian hybrid warfare' is widely understood as a method of operating that relies on proxies and surrogates to prevent attribution and intent and to maximize confusion and uncertainty. While conventional force is often obliquely mentioned, the main element of this Russian approach is that it remains below the threshold of the clear use of armed force.

Russian hybrid warfare is thus tantamount to a range of hostile actions of which military force is only a small part, measures that seek to deceive, undermine, subvert, influence and destabilize societies, to coerce or replace sovereign governments and to disrupt or alter an existing regional order. It emphasizes ambiguity in Russian action and is seen to provide Moscow with an asymmetric tool to undercut Western advantages. Its asymmetry has become a primary feature of the discussion, despite General Rupert Smith's pertinent observation that labelling wars as asymmetric is something of a 'euphemism to avoid acknowledging that my opponent is not playing to my strengths and I am not winning',[48] and it is seen to reflect Moscow's preference for measures short of war.

This subsequently became the foundation of much of the wider public policy and media debate about Russian actions, even as the situation in Ukraine evolved and Russia intervened in the Syrian civil war in autumn 2015. Debate focused on potential 'hybrid' threats to NATO and its member states, and planning scenarios developed which reflected a repeat of aspects of the Russian intervention in Ukraine and in the Baltic states. Such was the attention dedicated to hybrid warfare matters that departments have been established to address the challenge, a European Centre of Excellence for Countering Hybrid Threats was established (and inaugurated in October 2017 by Federica Mogherini and Jens Stoltenberg),[49] and senior figures appointed to deal with the challenge, such as an Ambassador for Hybrid Affairs.[50]

And Gerasimov did state that the 'role of non-military means has grown and in many cases exceeded the power of force of weapons in their effectiveness'. He also pointed to the roles of special operations forces and 'internal opposition to create a permanently operational front through the entire territory of the enemy state', and the blurring of the lines between war and peace.[51] And in early 2017, Moscow announced the establishment of information warfare units which were tasked, according to Russian Defence Minister Sergei Shoigu, with waging information warfare.[52]

Moreover, the term 'hybrid warfare' – which by the mid-2010s was largely synonymous with nefarious Russian activity – has served some useful purposes. It has, for instance, in some cases allowed NATO and its member states to discuss and build consensus about the challenges Russia poses without explicitly or officially naming Russia. It has also served as a mechanism for managing the debate about evolving security threats – it has helped, for example, to shift the focus of both analytical attention and bureaucratic resources beyond counter-terrorism and counter-insurgency that had dominated the Euro-Atlantic security agenda for much of the period since 2001.

Nevertheless, it is a misleading way of interpreting Russia and the challenge or threat that it poses. The term 'hybrid warfare' itself is not new, and the way it is attributed to Russian activity blurs and confuses rather than clarifies. Originally, hybrid warfare was defined as a combination of new technologies and fanatical fighting styles without state structures, uniforms or obedience to the laws of armed conflict.[53] Hybrid warfare was understood as the asymmetrical tactics of non-state or sub-state forces rather than their use by states – based on Western experience of counter-insurgency. But not only has it become detached from the original meaning: given how it is now applied to a state actor, 'hybrid warfare' has become so broad and diluted in its meaning as to be lost among all the other similar epithets, including 'grey zone', 'ambiguous warfare' and 'non-linear warfare'. As a result, it has lost the clarity that would make it useful. According to Robert Johnson, Director of the Oxford Changing Character of War Centre (CCW), therefore, this lack of definitional clarity means that all wars have contained elements of hybridity, and it also becomes indistinguishable from other manifestations of irregular, asymmetric or unconventional operations.[54]

Furthermore, if it has served to forge consensus, it has also become a trap for thinking. Language and discourse play an integral role in conflict, shaping and directing – or misdirecting – strategic theory and effort. As Jeff Michaels, Senior Lecturer at the UK's Defence Academy, has pointed out, though, political and military leaders can become trapped by the terminology they use, and become compelled to adopt policies and practices to justify or abide by their discourse. Equally, he notes, not only does the 'discourse trap' exclude other ways of defining the problems, but sheer repetition of the discourse can make it difficult for leaders to make a paradigm shift and escape from the constructs to deal with new circumstances.[55] This latter caution is relevant to understandings of 'Russian hybrid warfare'.

This is because it does not relate to Russian concepts.[56] Since the term became current in the Euro-Atlantic debate about Russia in 2014–15, Russian officials and observers have been emphatic that 'hybrid warfare' is not a Russian concept but a *Western* one, and it is something that is being waged against Russia. There is no Russian-language term to frame this, merely a transliteration ('gibridnaya voina') of the Western term. Indeed, a large part of the problem is that those who frame Russian activity in hybrid terms have done so without either Russian-language sources or detailed, empathetic consideration of the view from Moscow, or the Russian leadership's actual approach – and the many difficulties it faces. While a Russian strategy is often assumed and asserted, therefore, there is too big a gap between what the Euro-Atlantic community thinks it sees in Russian activities, and how the Russians themselves conceive them. Importantly, the discussion does not allow for difficulties in implementation, or the perennial 'fog' and 'friction' inherent in warfare.

The 'Gerasimov Doctrine' as it is understood in the Euro-Atlantic community does not exist. It serves, however, to illuminate problems that have beset the Euro-Atlantic community's thinking about Russian activity. As noted above, it is based on an article published under Gerasimov's name in early 2013. But this article contained thinking that reflected longer-term views that had already long before been taking shape, including under Gerasimov's predecessor, Nikolai Makarov, Russian Chief of General Staff from 2008 to 2012. If it could equally have been called the 'Makarov Doctrine', therefore, the point is that the history of and evolution in Russian military thinking were missed, and it remains to be seen what further confusions will happen when Gerasimov retires and his successor publishes articles.

Furthermore, only specific snippets from the article were used, and few if any of Gerasimov's many other subsequent writings or speeches have made any substantial impression on the Euro-Atlantic community's discussion about Russian thinking or activity. Yet his subsequent articles – 'On the Experience of Syria' and 'The World on the Brink of War', among others – shed important light on how the Russian military leadership sees the world. Similarly, rare are the attempts to relate Gerasimov's article to official Russian security and defence documents such as the National Security Strategy and Military Doctrine.

And, though a doctrine was named after him, who the man who had supposedly shaped this 'Doctrine' was, his background, his education and experience as an armoured warfare officer with service both in Chechnya and in military district command, and, importantly, his role in the wider Russian defence and security community, were missing.[57] Even years after the war in Ukraine began, many of those using the term knew almost nothing about the author of this supposed doctrine – symptomatic of a wider lack of understanding and lack of curiosity not just about Russian military theory, but also about the Russian armed forces and how they function.

Gerasimov's article was a response to the perceived evolution and changing character of war as led by others, particularly the US and its allies. As a result, asserting that Moscow had developed a new method of fighting allowed much confusion to seep into what was actually going on. On the one hand, there is a confusion about the level at which to frame Russian activity: it is often mistakenly portrayed as a *strategic* approach. But if the approach can be said to exist at all, the Russian leadership is clear: these are 'so called hybrid methods', in other words, *tactical*.

On the other hand, this masks the extent to which the Russian military has been trying to understand and adapt to, and even adopt, Western approaches to warfare. Discussion of 'Russian hybrid warfare' not only overlooks important aspects of Gerasimov's article, including how hybrid-type conflicts can evolve and merge, drawing states into interstate wars and the need therefore to develop a clear understanding of the forms and methods of the use and application of force.[58] It also stamps a formulaic label on Russian thinking that prevents more sophisticated understanding of the ongoing debates under way across the Russian military and security establishment about the changing character of war, wars of the future and the role of the military – and occasional references to the work of Sergei Chekinov and Sergei Bogdanov, two Russian authors who have written on asymmetric and information operations, and are sometimes recycled in much the same way as is Gerasimov's 2013 article, are an insufficient fig leaf. This is an important omission when Russian military thinking is evolving as a result of the acquisition of new equipment, the thousands of exercises conducted by the defence and security establishment, experience in Ukraine and much combat experience in Syria.

With these points in mind, third, thinking in these terms anchors Euro-Atlantic thinking about Russian activity to the annexation of Crimea, and the early period of the outbreak of war in Ukraine, even as conditions – and Russian actions – have evolved. Of course, the debates about hybrid warfare have themselves evolved considerably both in the Euro-Atlantic community and in Russia. But this has been in terms of adding new dimensions of hybridity, broadening it beyond usefulness, and a race to 'backdate' such 'hybrid' techniques. If Marie Yovanovitch, US ambassador to Ukraine, asserted that Russia has waged hybrid warfare against Ukraine for twenty-five years, long before the term came into currency, for instance, there are those in Moscow who assert that US hybrid-war-type techniques were used to bring down the USSR.[59]

But the debate largely takes the annexation of Crimea as its starting point, and this has come to be seen as a predictive doctrinal model for how Russian operations were going to be conducted. A particular point of attention is how a repetition of a Crimean-style hybrid offensive against a NATO member, particularly in the Baltic region, became the foundation scenario for thinking about a potential

Russian threat. Not only were Crimea and Eastern Ukraine very specific campaigning grounds, however, with unique geographic, political and cultural circumstances that are not readily applicable elsewhere, but that is not how the Russian leadership understands conflict. In his 2013 article, Gerasimov himself explicitly noted how each conflict is unique, with its own logic.[60]

Measures of War

Furthermore, the debate about 'Russian hybrid war' draws a veil over the conventional aspects of the war in Ukraine and the use of violent force in Russian military thinking. While non-military means of power were deployed in Ukraine, more traditional conventional measures were also visible, as shown in the battles of Debaltsevo, Donbass airport and Ilovaisk, during which much of the fighting involved high-intensity combat and the extensive use of armour, artillery and multiple-launch rocket systems, as well as drones and electronic warfare. During these battles, massed bombardments were deployed to lethal effect. At best, therefore, these so-called hybrid methods set the stage for the effective use of force in Ukraine; at worst, they failed, requiring the use of substantial conventional force.

Furthermore, the continuing central role of the use of violent force in Russian military thinking is illustrated by Russia's intervention in the war in Syria. Even as the focus on hybrid warfare was reaching a peak in the Euro-Atlantic discussion, Russian official statements emphasized the scale of (violent) force deployed to strike hundreds of targets, 'supplementing high intensity operations' with 'massive' strategic air raids, delivering 'powerful strikes' across Syria's territory. As Putin put it even in late 2015, Russia has conducted a 'comprehensive application of force ... allowing Russia qualitatively to change the situation in Syria', and a 'great deal has been done over the course of the past year to expand the potential of our armed forces ... Russia has reached a new level of operational use of its troops with a high readiness among units.'⁶¹ Since then, there has been considerable further movement as Moscow has tested new equipment and formations in the campaign. Importantly, Gerasimov himself has also pointed to the successful use of armed force to stop a hybrid-type, regime-change campaign. This is emphasized by Russia's military modernization programme, which includes the acquisition of much hardware and firepower.

The Hybrid Bias

None of this is intended to deny that 'hybrid warfare' or 'measures short of war' have something to say about methods of contemporary war. But it is to emphasize that this is not a *Russian* construction – there is not a '*Russian* hybrid war' in the way it is conceived – and that the use of the term builds in numerous confusions in the understanding of the challenge Russia poses. Most importantly for the argument in this book, the term introduces a hybrid bias that perpetuates an inaccurate view of Russian defence and security thinking. It warps understanding of Russian activity because it converts the tactical and operational into a strategic horizon – but with little or no connection to actual Russian strategy. Derived as it is from snapshots of Russian successes particularly in early 2014, it underlines 'measures short of war', and it blinds us to the failures of this approach in both 2014 and 2015, and the many changes in strategic realities since then. Most important of all, it distracts from the *measures of war*.

To return to the theme of learning from history, the dangers of partial and inflexible lesson learning are clear, and a vivid example is offered by Japanese forces in Manchuria in 1945. Japanese forces looked not at their experience of the battles of Khalkin Gol in 1939, including the Soviet 'penchant for doing the seemingly impossible', or the transformation of the Red Army between 1942 and 1945, but only at the Red Army's failures in the Finnish war and against the 1941 German invasion. Missing everything in

between, they were comprehensively taken by surprise and
defeated. Thus, according to David Glantz, the blindness
born of biases we bring to the study of Russia is a dangerous phenomenon that inhibits full understanding.[62]

Recalibrating the Russian Threat and the Need to Refresh Thinking

Concerns about Russian capabilities are not idle. They have
evolved significantly since 2008. Russian economic pressure, together with diplomatic, cyber and espionage capabilities, as well as information/disinformation campaigns,
can and do pose important questions and security challenges
for the Euro-Atlantic community.[63] But the way they are
depicted – particularly given the context of a loss of confidence – magnifies Russian capabilities, effectively asserting
the omniscience and omnipotence of the Russian leadership
(primarily Putin personally), and are contrasted directly
with Euro-Atlantic indecision, weakness and unprepared-
ness.[64] Thus Euro-Atlantic strengths – particularly those in
the cyber and informational domains – are masked, if not
completely ignored, as are Russian weaknesses, problems,
doubts and difficulties.

Russian propaganda and information/disinformation are
a prominent element of the Euro-Atlantic discussion, and
particularly the influence of Russian media outlets RT and
Sputnik. The report by the (US) Office of the Director of
National Intelligence suggested that 'Russia's state-run propaganda machine contributed to the influence campaign
by serving as a platform for Kremlin messaging to Russian
and international audiences.'[65] But while it has long been
clear, for instance, that Moscow seeks to advance its own
narrative, and has greatly improved its ability to do so
since the Russo–Georgia war in 2008, there are limits to
its influence across the Euro-Atlantic community. Observers
note RT's small audience. The American academic Ellen
Mickiewicz, for instance, has argued that while analysing

content may show RT's intentions, it does not show what its actual impact is. She also points out that RT was largely absent from US cable news rankings in 2015, and in Europe the audience is less than 0.1 per cent.[66]

Likewise, Russian cyber capabilities have grown considerably, but have limits. Adrien Chen, one of the first US journalists to report on the St Petersburg 'troll farm', the Internet Research Agency, is one of a group of reporters, including well-known critics of the Russian authorities, to emphasize that Russian efforts are often 'blown out of all proportion' as a kind of giant, sophisticated machine, a 'savvy, efficient manipulator of American public opinion', with little mention of the concomitant ineptitude and haphazard nature of their operations,[67] or the scale of investment in and skills of US political campaigners and cyber capabilities.

The Russian military offers a similar picture. Across the Euro-Atlantic community, there is concern about Russian remilitarization since the early 2010s. And it is true that the Russian leadership has invested heavily in the modernization of the Russian armed forces, with the result that by the mid-2010s, the military had once again become a deployable tool of national power, with the visible results of the campaign in Syria. Nevertheless, this warrants two notes of caution.

First, this burst of increased investment came after nearly three decades of very limited and poorly directed investment in the Russian armed forces. As Charles Dick, a British specialist on Soviet and Russian military affairs, wrote in 1998, the Russian Army had been 'in decline since before it came into existence – that is to say that the Soviet Army, its foundation, was increasingly in a state of disrepair as the Gorbachev era progressed'. After prolonged 'malign neglect', he continued, 'it is not merely ineffective ... it is on the verge of collapse ... the accumulated and deepening problems are formidable'.[68] The decline of the quality of the Russian armed forces into the 2000s was both the consequence of a sharp and extended decline in defence

spending, and because remaining spending was spread too
thinly across a poorly organized and deployed force.[69] While
there is an obvious improvement, therefore, during the last
few years, this is from a very low base, and progress remains,
in the words of one careful observer, 'fitful, unevenly dis-
tributed across the force, and with caveats and questions
about its future trajectory'.[70]

Second, it is worth noting the scale of spending. Clearly
a priority for the Russian leadership, Moscow has indeed
allocated considerable funds for defence modernization –
the plans in 2010 offered $640 billion, a substantial figure
when compared to that spent by many European militaries.
All told, this has facilitated a considerable modernization.
But it is worth comparing this to the defence expenditure
of other states. While Russia did indeed increase its defence
expenditure significantly between 2008 and 2017, so did
China, Turkey, Saudi Arabia and Australia. And by most
estimates, Russia has the fourth largest defence budget –
behind the USA, China and Saudi Arabia. Russia's ten-year,
one-off modernization programme is approximately the
same as US yearly military expenditure, and Russia's whole
yearly defence budget is smaller than just the increase insti-
gated by Donald Trump in February 2018. The US spends
more on defence than China and Russia combined, and
NATO allies France (sixth), the UK (seventh) and Germany
(ninth) are all in the top ten defence spenders.[71] Awareness
of the nature of Russian defence spending, therefore, should
not overshadow comparative realities.

To come to terms with this and respond effectively requires
a sophisticated and nuanced approach. Instead, thinking
is in the grip of exhausted metaphorical shorthand. This
mischaracterizes the challenges as they are evolving and
taking shape in the twenty-first century, introducing shibboleths and myths – not to say fantasies – to the debate.
It also calcifies an essentialist approach to Russia that hinders
the ability to discern Moscow's strengths and weaknesses,
as well as a clear understanding of the policy successes and
failures and disagreements of the last twenty-five years.

This shorthand has thus introduced rigidity and dogma to the first level of the security dilemma, that of interpretation, allowing a deceptively quick and easy skip to the second level of response.

Language matters. It can confuse and mislead, mischaracterizing the nature of the challenge. Much of the language in today's Euro-Atlantic debate about Russia and the challenges it poses would fail George Orwell's critique: he would surely have highlighted the staleness of imagery, the lack of precision and the loss of vividness. He might also have noted that the language used consists of dying (or already dead) metaphors, less and less of words chosen for the sake of their meaning and more and more of 'phrases tacked together like the sections of a prefabricated hen-house'.[72]

And History matters. But not, as Bew has colourfully put it, in the 'tendency to go at history like a looter at an archaeological site, indifferent to context and deeper meaning, concerned only with taking what can be immediately used or sold'.[73] Nor even does it matter in terms of the lessons that might be learnt: as we have seen, those who carefully study the lessons of last time without reflecting on change commit serious errors. It is about education and judgement, and understanding both continuity and change. History can make an important contribution. But to paraphrase Butterfield, if there has been much recent talk about avoiding the mistakes of Munich and 1938, in fact what are to be avoided in 2019 are not the mistakes of 1938, but the mistakes of 2019. Those who talk of avoiding the mistakes of 1938 are using history to ratify the prejudices they already have.[74] Or, to quote Abraham Lincoln, in his annual message to Congress in 1862, 'The dogmas of the quiet past, are inadequate to the stormy present ... As our case is new, so we must think anew, and act anew. We must disenthrall ourselves, and then we shall save our country.'

3

From Dialogue to Deterrence

If the dilemma of interpretation has been resolved for many, there has been an ongoing, evolving debate about the response. Some have argued that diplomacy should be used to cool the tension and seek points of common interest to develop cooperation. In January 2015, Federica Mogherini, emphasizing that there was no 'return to normal, no business as usual', also suggested that the EU should consider re-engaging with Russia. She argued that it would be 'useful' to add more diplomatic efforts to solving the crisis with Russia, as well as both political dialogue on global and regional issues such as Syria, the Iran nuclear deal, the Middle East peace process and a technical dialogue on energy.[1] The intention was to attempt to build a proactive approach to 'break the impasse over Ukraine and halt a downward spiral of hostility with a huge neighbour that is both powerful and facing economic difficulty'. Such a re-engagement would include carrots as well as sticks, trade-offs and a give-and-take approach that could include resumption of efforts to allow visa-free travel between Russia and the EU, and negotiations towards a new framework for EU–Russia relations.[2] Speaking at the St Petersburg International Economic Forum, Jean-Claude Juncker stated that we must talk with Russia ... the illegal annexation of Crimea and Sevastopol, and the conflict in and around eastern Ukraine put the relations between the EU and Russia to a severe test. Russia's actions have shaken the very principles of the European security order. Sovereign equality, the non-use of force and territorial integrity matter. ... But if our relationship today is troubled and marked by mistrust, it is not broken beyond repair. We need to mend it ... when our relations are tense, we must keep talking. Even when economic sanctions are in place, we must keep the door open. And ... I want to build a bridge.[3]

In the US, there has also been also talk of 'reviving détente' or a 'Détente Plus' approach. Though this would not overlook serious disagreements, nevertheless transnational terrorism, threats from civil wars, failed states and rogue groups gaining possession of weapons of mass destruction are seen by some to be threats common to both the US and Russia, warranting a more cooperative approach. According to some, therefore, there is a need for 'nuance and syncopation against a steady drumbeat bringing these two countries to conflict', and the goal should be a 'realistic security partnership', one that acknowledges that there have been 'fumbles' by both parties.[4]

This 'Détente Plus' approach would involve developing a diplomatic strategy with leverage, one that 'retains the sanctions regime and credible prospects for a NATO presence until its benefits materialize'. Such a strategy would be based on treating Russia as 'a great power that possesses real and legitimate interests, especially in its border areas'. This would 'not treat Russia as an enemy but as a combination of adversary and partner' as a means of addressing important political matters in Europe and worldwide, 'recognising the range of common and overlapping interests' to establish meaningful cooperation. Treating Russia this way would gain leverage with which to 'tame Russian assertiveness and secure Russia's restraint on its western border, and step up joint action based on common interests on other critical fronts such as terrorism, Syria, Iran and nuclear proliferation'.[5]

Against this many have advocated deterrence, indeed that deterrence should come *instead* of dialogue. The idea of dialogue with Russia is criticized for its association with Munich-type appeasement, resulting in a compromise with Russia based on a desire to set aside differences over Ukraine to resume profitable business. Toomas Hendrik Ilves, President of Estonia until 2016, for instance, stated that Russia should be 'deterred, not communicated with', rejecting the idea that dialogue can be developed while strengthening deterrence. 'Dialogue is not a policy, deterrence is a policy', he argued.[6] Likewise, Lithuanian Foreign Minister Linas Linkevicius stated that 'détente would not work with Russia this time'. Seeking to re-establish dialogue with Moscow was based on wishful thinking, he suggested, and would demonstrate that the West had learned nothing from Moscow's aggression in Georgia and Ukraine. In attempting to renew dialogue and cooperation with Russia, the West was 'beginning the ancient game of reconciliation and warming relations'. Not only does this mean that the West 'assumes the blame for the worsening of relations' with Russia, he suggested, it also would be received in Moscow as a 'sign of weakness and an additional opportunity, even stimulus for Moscow to act still more energetically'.[7] And since the US presidential elections in late 2016, there has been an emphatic shift towards the need for deterrence in Washington, DC. This chapter explores these approaches, reflecting first on the debate about dialogue before turning to examine that about deterrence.

'Not Back to Business as Usual'

One of the stock phrases in the Euro-Atlantic debate about how to deal with Russia is that while it is important to engage with Russia, there should be no return to 'business as usual' after the annexation of Crimea. As Michael Fallon, then the UK's Secretary of Defence, put it in July 2017, 'we have to engage with Russia. That cannot be business as usual with Russia while Crimea remains annexed and while Ukraine is being interfered with. But we think it important to have a dialogue with Russia to try and de-escalate any tensions that there are.'[8]

The phrase 'not back to business as usual' has served a number of purposes. It seeks to suggest that the Euro-Atlantic community has 'learnt' the diplomatic lessons of the Russo–Georgia war in 2008 after which Russia, many argue, was not suitably punished. It also illustrates the lack of trust and self-confidence, and that engagement and business as usual might be seen to compromise the punishment for Ukraine.

But it invites an obvious retort: what was 'business as usual'? A return to business as usual would be a return to a relationship that was stagnating, replete with mutual frustration and disagreements. To be sure, the war in Ukraine has created a new, more adversarial context, compounded by the mutual accusations of interference in domestic politics, and the war in Syria. But the war in Ukraine was less a crisis than a paroxysm.

Indeed, relations between the Euro-Atlantic community and Russia have been stuck in an increasingly systemic dissonance since the early 2000s. Though there were important disagreements in the 1990s – most notably NATO's campaign in the former Yugoslavia and Kosovo in 1999 – the period 2002–4 was a turning point, after which the intention to establish a 'strategic partnership' with Russia faded.

There was some practical cooperation, and mechanisms for dialogue were established, such as the NATO–Russia Council (NRC) in 2002, and EU–Russia Permanent Partnership Council meetings began in 2003. But large parts of the agenda for cooperation remained unfulfilled, and a number of political and security disagreements dominated relations. These included NATO enlargement, the colour revolutions, particularly in Georgia and Ukraine, the disagreements over the Treaty on Conventional Forces in

Europe (CFE) and Russia's unilateral suspension of it in 2007, the Russo–Georgia war in 2008, and the energy disputes between Gazprom and Naftogaz Ukraini in 2006 and 2009. These disagreements served to emphasize the other problems in the relationship, such as the divergence in values, including the Euro-Atlantic community's criticism of Russian actions during the war in Chechnya, the Yukos Oil Company case, and other criticisms of Moscow's human rights and democratic record. Moscow has reciprocated. The Russian leadership has long been explicit in its assertions of Euro-Atlantic double standards, rejected Euro-Atlantic liberal values, and advocated the need to defend what it sees as traditional values even against a Euro-Atlantic threat to them.[9]

If Euro-Atlantic observers characterized relations as being in 'depression' by 2008, Russians agreed. By 2010, as Timofei Bordachev, Associate Professor at the Higher School of Economics in Moscow, put it, the EU–Russia relationship had become characterized by a 'firmly entrenched stagnation', caused by the failure of institutions and practices to adapt to contemporary challenges and an outdated agenda. Moscow's attitude to the EU and its foreign policy actions, he argued, was 'increasingly characterised by exasperation, verging on open distrust', particularly regarding the EU's Eastern Partnership programme, which the Russian leadership saw as competing in the former Soviet space. Despite increasing trade, economic and cultural connections, therefore, 'systemic stagnation' was caused by an extended sense of inertia and a lack of clear strategic goals.[10] Much the same could be said of the NATO–Russia relationship as the areas for practical cooperation contracted sharply, and disagreements increased.

Likewise, relations between Washington and London and Moscow were stuck in a systemic dissonance well before the war in Ukraine. US–Russia relations are widely covered elsewhere and the headline tensions need little re-emphasis here, but two points stand out in terms of 'business as usual' and dialogue. First, as Angela Stent has pointed out, there have already been four attempts to 'reset' the US–Russia relationship in the post-Cold War era. Though these have occasionally generated positive results, such as agreement on a new Strategic Arms Reduction Treaty (START) signed in 2010, and a supply route for coalition troops in Afghanistan, there has been an overall long-term deterioration in relations since well before 2014. Disagreements over the use of force to change regimes without the sanction of the UN meant that relations began to 'fray' from 2002 and became 'increasingly polarised'. The Obama reset was effectively finished before the end of his first term in 2013: disagreements over Libya, Syria and Russia's granting of asylum to Edward Snowden compounded the longer-term disagreements over the Iraq war, NATO enlargement, Ballistic Missile Defence (BMD), the US Freedom Agenda, Russian democratization and governance, among others, such that a summit scheduled for September 2013 was cancelled, and Obama called for a pause in relations to reassess Russia's direction and what US core interests were.

Second, there has been considerable continuity in the substance of relations, regardless of the administration. There is a long and challenging list of issues that both sides have had to confront, Stent notes, but 'it has been a constant challenge for Washington to move forward on a constructive and productive agenda with Russia', and 'in view of the differences between the Russian and US political systems and world views, the range of possible ways of dealing with these issues is limited'. She tellingly quotes Putin, who, following discussions with Obama in 2013, stated that 'we hear each other and understand the arguments. But we simply do not agree. I do not agree with his arguments and he does not agree with mine.'[11]

Relations between London and Moscow have similarly been troubled since the early 2000s. There has been some noteworthy practical cooperation. The UK played a prominent role in raising the sunken Russian AS28 submersible in 2005, for instance, and has contributed to a range of practical cooperative projects in Russia, such as the disposal of nuclear submarines, the retraining of servicemen, and infrastructure design and construction, including in public transport and flood protection barrier projects. There has also been some substantial mutual trade and investment, including in the energy sector.[12]

But a wide range of disagreements, in both global affairs and bilateral relations,[13] have been exacerbated by a series of specific crises, including Litvinenko's murder in 2006, which resulted in the suspension of much practical cooperation, and a number of spy scandals, such as the 'spy rock' episode – also in 2006. The energy crises of 2006 and 2009, and the Russo–Georgia war in 2008, emphasized the political and security dissonance between London and Moscow, characterized by the UK House of Commons Defence Committee as *Russia: A New Confrontation?*[14] And having grown considerably from 2004, the economic relationship peaked in 2008 and then sharply contracted. High-level dialogue also contracted to a trickle.

Though David Cameron sought to reinvigorate the relationship between 2010 and 2014, results were mixed. The economic relationship recovered slowly in 2010–12, but has been in decline since. And the Litvinenko case remained a central feature of relations, which were regularly punctuated by more extradition and spy scandals, and the disagreements over Libya and Syria. Even before the outbreak of war in Ukraine, therefore, 'business as usual' was a very difficult business.

No Grand Bargain

Though officials point to common interests, such as international terrorism, the disagreements are many, and the mechanisms for dialogue either suspended or operating infrequently – such as at the NRC – only to rehearse differences. The disagreements range from the local to the regional and beyond, and it is difficult to see where substantive breakthroughs might be made. The Euro-Atlantic community and Russia approach the situation in Syria at odds in terms of the causes of the war and the conduct of the campaigns, including whom to support and whom to target (and consequently have each levelled severe accusations against the other), and what the outcome should be.

A similar situation prevails in the war in Ukraine, where the positions of the sides, particularly between Washington (and London) and Moscow are diametrically at odds over the causes and blame for and the conduct of the war. Though a second peace plan, Minsk II, was agreed in February 2015, and there are mechanisms for dialogue, including special envoys, the situation is well characterised as a 'stalemate'.[15] The Minsk II agreement contains many difficulties, particularly for Ukraine, since it was agreed in the wake of a series of military defeats. Though it is specific about the sequence of the provisions, the two sides cannot agree on who should make the first move (though exchanges of prisoners have occurred). While Euro-Atlantic officials and observers assert their 'very strong sense of disappointment and frustration in Washington that Russia has done absolutely nothing to end the conflict or to withdraw its forces', Russians assert that the responsibility is in Kyiv, that there would be no progress without political agreements, but that Moscow could not sign the amnesty law adopted by the Ukrainian parliament.[16] According to some, the decision in December 2017 to provide Ukraine with lethal weapons 'amounts to the death of Minsk', since military action has now replaced diplomacy, and a turn towards 'muddling through without a roadmap from now on'.[17]

Connected to the situation in Ukraine, two other important related questions linger, both the source of much disagreement and mutual recriminations: the first concerns arms control, the second the broader Euro-Atlantic security architecture. Both lie at the heart of the post-Cold War relationship and reflect the divergent understandings of security. The two are closely linked: as one report has suggested, Moscow sees the security order as 'rigged in favour of the Euro-Atlantic organizations. It is actively seeking to establish an alternative order that would grant Moscow a sphere of privileged interests in its "near abroad".' The US, on the other hand, seeks to uphold the existing agreements, pointing to Russia's behaviour as the cause of the European security problems. 'Arms control is thus only meaningful as long as it is embedded in a rules-based security order.'[18]

Arms control agreements have been under pressure for much of the last twenty years – from the US unilateral withdrawal from the ABM Treaty to Russia's unilateral suspension of the CFE Treaty – partly as a result of the failure to ratify the Adapted CFE Treaty and the US missile defence programme – and then subsequent withdrawal from it in 2015. Though some senior European officials have argued for a reinvigoration of arms control and transparency as a means of limiting unintended escalation, this has not received unanimous support from across the Euro-Atlantic community. Observers note that the prospects for negotiations on a new conventional arms control regime are 'slim', and the legally and politically binding documents are endangered because Moscow sees them as 'anathema to its national security interests'.[19]

Indeed, observers and officials on both sides point to the possible end of the arms control regimes. Washington and Moscow exchange accusations of violation of the Intermediate-Range Nuclear Forces (INF) Treaty, with both threatening to withdraw from the agreement.[20] As Eugene Rumer has put it, 'the significance of this development for arms control overall is hard to overestimate ... the new START treaty ratified in 2011 is likely to be the last arms control treaty between Russia and the US for a long time to come', and both countries face an uphill struggle if they are to preserve the INF Treaty and New START, which is due to expire in 2021.[21]

The wider Euro-Atlantic security architecture is a source of long-standing contention. If Russian opposition to specific Euro-Atlantic policies, including NATO enlargement and the BMD programme, is the most obvious feature of this, underpinning it is a bigger conceptual question about how the map of Europe has been redrawn over the last twenty five years. This includes debates over the indivisibility of security in Europe and equality in decision-making. If the Euro-Atlantic goal was a 'Europe whole, free and at peace', Moscow argued that it was 'fragmented, bound by bloc mentality and riven by conflict', and bound by obsolete architectures and mechanisms. Thus in 2008, Moscow proposed a reconsideration of the Euro-Atlantic security architecture, and the development of a new treaty. (This was in fact part of a three-pronged approach that proposed debate and renewal of the security, energy and financial architectures.) Russian officials used the language of 'Greater Europe', and reflected on the need for a new version of the European Coal and Steel Community, symbolic as it was of tying France and Germany together at their roots to ensure security. Russian observers thus argued that Moscow sought a peace treaty to end the Cold War. The following year, Moscow offered a draft treaty.

This resulted in the Corfu Process. But the approaches of the two sides could hardly have been more different: the Euro-Atlantic community rejected Moscow's proposals on practical grounds (as insufficiently developed) and conceptually, stating their opposition to Russia establishing a 'sphere of influence' or of 'privileged interest', reaffirming their commitment to existing structures, including the CFE, and condemning Russian recognition of South Ossetia and Abkhazia. Moscow's proposals remain the conceptual underpinning of Russian foreign policy in Europe – and the debate continues to divide the two sides, with the Euro-Atlantic community rejecting any idea of a 'new Yalta', supposedly signifying the big powers dividing up the world into spheres of influence.[22] This wide range of practical and conceptual disagreements mean that striking some 'grand bargain' will be extremely difficult.

Despite these disagreements and the sanctions, points of contact remain. There is a hotline for deconflicting military activities in Syria: according to one report, US officials stated it was being used ten to twelve times each day in summer 2017. While the phone calls have been 'tense', according to one senior military officer, the Iraq-based commander of the US coalition forces, Lieutenant General Stephen Townsend, stated that the Russians have been 'nothing but professional, cordial and disciplined'.[23] NATO's SACEUR, General Scaparrotti, met Gerasimov in Baku in April 2018,[24] and senior US military officials have also been in contact with Gerasimov in specific deconfliction roles, including a meeting between Generals Dunford and Gerasimov in Finland in June 2018. Other examples of ongoing contact also stand out: in an extraordinary development, given the wider nature of the relationship and sanctions, the heads of Russian security and intelligence services, Alexander Bortnikov, Igor Korobov and Sergey Naryshkin, were invited to Washington in January 2018.[25]

But Russia remains a toxic subject across the wider US political landscape. Despite the ongoing presidential connections, and the visits of John Bolton and a Congressional Delegation visit to Russia in June 2018, few currently appear inclined to advocate a major re-engagement with Russia. Indeed, the Countering America's Adversaries Through Sanctions Act (CAATSA) was passed 419–3 in the House of Representatives and 98–2 in the Senate, and not only has a double impact on the current situation – expanding the sanctions regime and limiting the current presidential administration's ability to negotiate – but also affects future administrations. The CAATSA thus has long-term implications for relations with Russia.

The UK has far less contact with Moscow. The UK's Vice Chief of Defence, General Gordon Messenger, met Colonel General Alexander Zhuravlyov in Moscow in February 2017.[26] According to the Russian Ministry of Defence, the meeting was held in a constructive manner and both sides agreed to continue interaction. Subjects discussed included the condition of and prospects for the renewal of military interaction, the situation in crisis regions and possible steps to prevent incidents during military activities. But this does not seem to have subsequently blossomed, and though then

Foreign Secretary Boris Johnson visited Moscow in December 2017, in the wake of events in Salisbury in March 2018 high-level contacts between the UK and Russia, already limited and tenuous, were suspended.

All told, though there are common interests, policy disagreements and conflicts of interest significantly curtail the extent to which these offer grounds for substantive engagement – and attempting to jump over old problems to start a forward-looking dialogue, or over local or regional problems to cooperate on wider international ones, does not offer substantial prospects. This will mean that 'engagement' remains limited to deconfliction and technical cooperation on the fringes, including maritime search and rescue[27] and in space,[28] but which is accurately characterized by one official as 'discussion, not cooperation'.

The Difficulties of Dialogue with Russia: the Example of Japan–Russia Relations

The Russian leadership often criticizes the Euro-Atlantic community both for 'dictate not dialogue' – 'formulating what it wants and then demanding implementation of its instructions' – and for being the party that suspended dialogue. Moscow also emphasizes its readiness to resume dialogue, and that cooperation has reaped rewards in the past, such as the Iran nuclear deal. But even given a sustained decision to return to substantive dialogue and engagement with Russia, this will not be easy. Any resumption will meet an extensive list of trenchantly held grievances and Russian positions with which the Euro-Atlantic community does not agree. As Putin has put it, the 'parties should act like partners and take in to account each other's interests. We are ready for this', and 'we are ready for dialogue, but dialogue is a search for compromise'.[29]

The example of Japanese Prime Minister Shinzo Abe's attempt to improve relations with Russia is indicative of the possibilities, challenges, limits and contradictions. Since he came to power in 2012, Abe has consistently sought to

improve relations, with the signing of a final peace treaty
from World War II and the resolution of the dispute over
the Northern Territories (known in Russian as the Southern
Kuriles) as the key goals.

As a member of the G7, Japan imposed sanctions on
Russia in the wake of the war in Ukraine. But in May
2016, Tokyo moved to normalize relations with a 'new
approach' to Russia. This was a break with the rest of the
G7, apparently against the advice of the US, and reflected
Japan's position that further isolating Russia could lead to
closer relations between Russia and China. The 'new
approach', according to senior Japanese officials, was
intended to offer a 'future oriented' approach to relations,
and, among other measures such as a relaxation of visa
regulations, included an eight-point plan for economic
cooperation with Russia. This included the offer of cooperation on infrastructure and urban development (including
ports, airports and hospitals), health and life expectancy
issues, energy (such as liquefied natural gas plants), and
promoting industrial diversification and the development
of cutting-edge technology.[30]

But linking economic cooperation to political negotiations has not reaped the rewards for which Tokyo hoped.
Moscow has appeared enthusiastic to develop economic
relations, and there have been numerous visits from senior
Russian officials, including Gerasimov, Yuri Trutnev, Arkadi
Dvorkovich, Sergei Naryshkin and Nikolai Patrushev. But
all this – and twenty-one meetings between Putin and Abe
– have not led to substantial progress for Tokyo's priorities.
Despite the broader dialogue, by May 2018 there was no
meaningful progress on either the peace treaty or the territorial dispute. Indeed, the Russian leadership has explicitly
stated that it does not link economic cooperation to these
issues,[31] reinforced its military presence on the Kurile islands,
and unilaterally declared a special economic zone on the
islands. Despite Tokyo's significant efforts, therefore, and
while dialogue has grown, the main goals have not been
achieved.[32] And if Japanese media are criticizing the Abe

effort for failing, Russian observers note that Moscow never gave any grounds for inflated expectations of the effort.[33]

The Shift to Deterrence

These protracted disagreements, combined with the strong renewed sense of threat, have led to an emphasis on deterring Russia. But if engagement in dialogue poses challenges, deterrence is not necessarily an easier option. It weaves together all the various features discussed above, from the security dilemma/security paradox continuum, to the Euro-Atlantic community's loss of confidence, to the labels and analogies explored in chapter 2.

The foundation of this approach has been, as officials and politicians have asserted, that the alliance needed to restore the credibility of its deterrence posture in the eyes of the Russian leadership, to protect the sovereignty and independence of its member states and deter further efforts to revise the status quo. By demonstrating firmness and consistency, the alliance should communicate the message to Moscow that the costs of any aggression would be so high that they would outweigh the benefits. The thrust of the debate has been to move, as illustrated by NATO's July 2016 Warsaw summit, 'from reassurance to deterrence'.

In the US, also, there is a strong emphasis on the need to deter Russia. The language of some in Washington has been vivid, with calls to 'tame' and 'defeat' Putin, as observers have advocated the need for a combination of deterrence, strengthening allies and partners and communicating the truth about Russian activity, and 'thwarting' Putin by 'fostering democracy' in Ukraine to undermine Putin's legitimacy in Russia. Indeed, the key to deterring and potentially changing Russia is Ukraine, according to one.[34] This opens up many questions that lie at the heart of deterrence.

The first point is about the cause of the Russia challenge, where there is a noteworthy – if often subtle – shift in the discussion between dialogue and deterrence. Despite the well known list of contemporary policy disagreements, when it comes to shaping deterrence, the focus on Russian behaviour shifts back towards essentialist views of Russian imperialism or towards it being an ideological question. Few, if any, of the discussions about defending Europe examine the circumstances that might lead to a Russian invasion of the Baltic states or why such a war might break out, relying instead on supposed historical analogy and assertions about Russian domestic considerations that are alleged to drive Moscow's foreign policy. Thus the threat is framed as Russian foreign policy adventurism, an unprovoked strike from a clear blue sky, rather than war erupting as miscalculation or the result of a sudden deterioration or crisis over a clash of policies.

According to Alexander Vershbow, then NATO Deputy Secretary General, the Russian threat is because of 'Russia's drive to define itself culturally in opposition to what it portrays as decadent western values – as a smoke screen for suppression of freedom and civil society at home'.[35] Others argue that Russian foreign policy is based on internal problems, especially flagging popular support for Putin because of a lack of democratic legitimacy and few prospects for economic modernization. In this view, Putin conducts foreign adventures such as the seizure of Crimea to maintain domestic support, or seeks to undermine and discredit the West to show that it does not offer an alternative.

Such views not only discount policy disagreements as a cause of war but oversimplify the Russian domestic political situation and ignore the absence of a tradition of 'short victorious wars' in Russian thinking. These views are widely held, and lie at the heart of the opinion that the current sharp deterioration in relations stems in the main from Putin's return to the presidency in 2012. Evelyn Farkas, a former defence official now with the Atlantic Council, for instance, asserts that because of the fall in oil prices and domestic corruption, his 'bargain' with the Russian people was no longer sustainable – and thus he adopted a nationalist, revisionist and anti-US foreign policy.[36]

The second point is that the discussion about deterring Russia is influenced by internal political debates about the role of the Euro-Atlantic community and especially the US in international affairs. Putin's supposed strength and decisiveness are directly contrasted with the vacillation and weakness of Euro-Atlantic leaders, who have 'failed to respond adequately or forcefully' and 'propose weak half measures'. Indeed, some argue that the 'West has shown a level of incompetence that approaches impotence', and in so doing 'abdicated the moral high ground on human rights, peaceful international co-existence and liberal democracy'.[37]

If the first point serves to frame Russia in a vacuum, rather than as part of a dynamic and evolving exchange based on policy disagreements and an evolving international context, this second serves as a foundation for asserting a forthright set of policy recommendations to 'do more', justified by myths and sacred tales. Thus a range of proposals to 'show strength' have been made, from establishing no-fly zones in Syria, to asserting US values, reforming and expanding NATO to 'capture the dynamism of so-called New Europe' (including Georgia and Ukraine), and supplying weapons to Ukraine – often regardless of international developments of the last fifteen years.[38]

There are complexities to this, such as the demands of political campaigning. Yet much of the debate about the need to assert strength, for instance, has appeared as criticism of the weakness, even cowardice of President Obama. The most obvious example is Obama's decision not to enforce the red line on the use of chemical weapons in Syria in 2013, which some assert gave Putin a 'green light' to annex Crimea shortly after in the knowledge that there would not be serious consequences.[39]

But if assertions about the supposed loss of US credibility because of its failure to punish Syria – leading subsequently to the 'green light in Crimea' – are of a piece with the Euro-Atlantic community's wider loss of confidence, they are highly problematic. Such assertions include little or no reflection on the consequences of the possible failure of punishment strikes, had they been carried out, or the possibility of being drawn into a protracted commitment to waging war in Syria (in the wake of the wars in Iraq and Afghanistan), and whether either of these eventualities would have weakened the resolve, credibility and, importantly, capability of the Euro-Atlantic community to respond to aggression elsewhere. Furthermore, it asserts credibility as related to reputation, and thus breaks with deterrence theory that suggests that credibility is not always enhanced by the use of military power – indeed that such use can be unnecessary and counterproductive. Equally, particular circumstances, levels of interest and capabilities that can be deployed are more important than credibility.[40]

Importantly, it is also a parochial, self-focused view: it does not consider how others viewed the decision to not intervene. In the case of the 'Syrian red line/Crimean green light', Russian observers and officials have been clear that there was no link between the US decision to not bomb Syria and Russian intervention the following year in Ukraine. Moscow's calculations were based on the specific circumstances – such as Ukraine's non-membership of NATO – rather than a lack of US punishment of Assad. Indeed, some suggested that Moscow saw the US decision not to intervene as an 'unusual moment of reason' that led to a US–Russia diplomatic agreement. For Moscow, therefore, it was US actions in Ukraine, rather than in Syria, that led to Russian actions in Ukraine.[41]

Deterrence or Reassurance?

One of the first measures that some consider to contribute to deterrence was the introduction of a range of sanctions by the US and EU on Russia in 2014. This did not result in a reversal of Moscow's policies, but some suggest that it served to restrain further Russian activity. The emphasis on developing defence-related deterrence also began in 2014, taking formal shape at NATO's summit in Wales in

September 2014, at which the alliance emphasized collective defence and deterrence and approved the Readiness Action Plan (RAP), designed to 'respond to the challenges posed by Russia and their strategic implications', and ensure that NATO remains 'strong, ready, robust and responsive'. In the longer term, the declaration stated the aim for member states to meet the guideline of a minimum spending of 2 per cent of gross domestic product (GDP) on defence, 20 per cent of which should be spent on major new equipment including research and development over the coming decade.

More immediately, the declaration stated the intention to establish a continuous, rotational presence of NATO forces in the eastern part of the alliance, as part of 'the fundamental baseline requirement for assurance and deterrence' that is both 'flexible and scalable' in response to the evolving security situation. It also includes measures to strengthen NATO's rapid reaction capabilities with the establishment of the VJTF, designed to be deployable within days to meet challenges at NATO's periphery and for reinforcement of member states for deterrence and collective defence. Importantly, the RAP included the need to establish 'appropriate command and control presence and some in-place force enablers' as well as the 'preparation of infrastructure, prepositioning of equipment and supplies and the designation of bases'.[42] This has resulted in the eFP, with multinational battalions deployed in Estonia, Latvia, Lithuania and Poland, eight new small headquarters in the eastern part of NATO, and numerous exercises. By 2015, NATO had also developed a strategy for dealing with hybrid threats.[43]

The NATO summit in Warsaw in 2016 sought to enhance this approach, including a range of measures to bolster security in the Black Sea region and framed cooperation with the EU. This cooperation – long problematic – was considered to be critical, and requiring new impetus and substance. Areas for cooperation include bolstering resilience; information and intelligence sharing; cooperation on strategic communication and response; broader, better cooperation in cyber security, and coordination in exercises, including dealing with hybrid threats.

It has also spurred the reversal of the withdrawal of US forces from Europe and a debate about the size, capability and future of the US Army. In April 2016, for instance, H. R. McMaster, a now retired US Army officer widely considered to be a thought leader and innovator in military affairs, and who went on to become US National Security Advisor from February 2017 to April 2018, stated that the shrinking size of the US Army, combined with its lack of modernization, created risks. He pointed to concerns about increasing obsolescence of US armour against modern anti-tank weapons, as well as Russian (and Chinese) capabilities in terms of electronic and cyber warfare and also layered systems of radars and anti-aircraft missiles. Such capabilities could mean that the US Army would potentially lose air support and be reliant on its own artillery, which is both outranged by Russian and Chinese equipment and vulnerable to command and control disruption through electronic and cyber means. Russian ability to shut down Ukrainian networks had been a 'wake-up call' for the US, particularly since US electronic warfare capabilities were disbanded in the 1990s. Having technological advantages in aerospace and cyber domains had meant that the US could use smaller forces; losing technological dominance, McMaster suggested, increases the importance of the size of the army.[44]

The US has adopted a leading role in seeking to establish deterrence through defence capability. Washington has quadrupled funding from $789 million in 2016 to $3.4 billion in 2017 in what was initially called the European Reassurance Initiative, and is now called the European Deterrence Initiative. This was established to focus funding specifically on measures to deter Russia, including munitions and prepositioned stocks, improving equipment and training and exercising. It additionally supports the continuous presence of a US armoured brigade combat team in Romania and Bulgaria.[45]

The US has also carried out numerous exercises. These have included the very short notice Freedom Shock exercises, which seek to train and sustain readiness to deploy at a moment's notice; Saber Strike, the annual international exercise led by the US Army Europe focused on the Baltic states; and the B2 and B52 bomber training missions, intended to demonstrate the 'ability to forward deploy and deliver conventional and nuclear deterrence anytime, anywhere' and the US long-range global strike capability.[46]

And in Northern European states, there has been much activity, including a significant increase in defence-related spending in the Baltic region (doubling between 2014 and 2018, and expected to increase further by 2020), redrafting of military strategies with new definitions of the security environment, and new taskings and deployments for the armed forces. Civilian volunteer militias and 'Home' and 'Youth' guards have become popular, with partisan warfare training events, and Lithuania reintroduced conscription in March 2016.

If there is much activity under way, however, there are three main caveats that are worth noting. The first is the conceptual shift from reassurance to deterrence. Though they are related, these are two different conversations with different audiences. There is a visible blurring in NATO and US terminology in the description of moving 'from reassurance to deterrence', as the journey from the Wales to the Warsaw summit is called. Deterrence of Russia will not be achieved by simply rebadging reassurance activities already under way as 'deterrence'. This may be further blurred by the debate about a move towards a 'from deterrence to defence' posture – in other words treating deterrence as only a political signal, compared to a credible defensive posture. As one senior European official noted, however, while politicians are content to discuss deterrence, few want to discuss defence.[47]

The second caveat regards ongoing internal problems and outstanding questions. Some of the decisions of Warsaw remain unfulfilled. Though the EU and NATO have much scope for cooperation and the staffs work together, relations are still complicated by long-standing political problems. Also, there is so much activity, with so many initiatives – such as the Joint Expeditionary Force (JEF), the Combined Joint Expeditionary Force (CJEF) and the European Intervention Initiative,[48] as well as NATO's VJTF – that questions may be asked about efficiency, resourcing and whether they are complementary or competitive.

Moreover, if there are still gaps in equipment, questions also remain about the sustainability of expensive exercises and constant readiness, and a range of logistical challenges.[49] Indeed, the issue of freedom of movement within the Euro-Atlantic area is difficult. There are shortages in transportation and infrastructure, in terms of either road, bridge or railway to transport heavy equipment. Furthermore, according to Hodges,[50] the bureaucratic processes for moving armed forces across Europe pose a significant obstacle to large-scale movements: they are tailored to a different reality from the contemporary challenge. It can take weeks to carry out a planned move – when it is important to be able to respond quickly to an emergent crisis. Ideas to address this are being advanced, by the Netherlands among others, with proposals including an idea to sign a 'mobility pledge' to cut red tape in order to grant permission as quickly as possible for military transport to cross borders and so shorten response times.[51]

The third caveat is about the consequences of the measures. It is questionable whether the sanctions indeed 'restrained' Russia from further activity. But despite some disruption, particularly in terms of access to finance, in macro terms their economic impact has so far been limited.[52] They illustrate a dual set of consequences. On the one hand, Moscow has countered by imposing retaliatory sanctions, which have had a negative effect on the economies of a number of EU states. On the other, Moscow has moved to develop its own resilience to such measures. As the British academic and specialist on Russian economics Julian Cooper suggested, therefore, the outcome of sanctions could 'turn out to be contrary to original intentions', Russia, he argued in 2014, may well 'emerge as a country with a military production capability almost immune to any future attempts by outside powers to cripple it'.[53] All of these caveats reinforce the point that deterrence should be part of a wider strategy, one in which coordination, forward planning and consequence management are essential. It also leads to the broader question of what is deterrence, as opposed to reassurance or political rhetoric.

What is Deterrence?

While there is much activity under way, observers and officials point to an important problem: the Euro-Atlantic community has difficulty conceptualizing deterrence. True, deterrence can be quite simply defined as the threat of force to discourage an opponent from taking unwelcome action. But for most of the post-Cold War era it has been viewed as a 'Cold War relic', and '20 years of neglect have taken their toll. Much of what was once considered basic knowledge on deterrence appears to have evaporated.' And mistakes in applying deterrence, Richard Betts argued, come from 'misunderstandings about the concept itself, forgetfulness about history, faulty threat assessments and short-sighted policy-making'.[54]

This creates a series of problems that complicate the Euro-Atlantic debate about deterrence. As NATO official Michael Rühle stated, deterrence is at times a necessary or useful instrument of policy, but the correct and prudent use of deterrence is by no means self-evident or easily determined in all circumstances. Though deterrence is currently being advocated as a catch-all solution to what is a complex situation with Russia, it should be remembered that there is no guarantee of success: deterrence can fail and often has failed, even with a weaker side attacking the stronger. The Argentinian invasion of the Falkland Islands in 1982 exemplifies this, illustrating the whole complex of reasons for deterrence failure: a lack of knowledge and understanding of the party to be deterred, particularly decision making (in the UK there was very limited defence intelligence focus on Argentina), and unclear messaging and interpretation. The withdrawal of HMS *Endurance* after the 1981 defence review was interpreted by Argentina as a signal of decreasing support for – and thus lack of willingness to defend – the Falklands, rather than the cost-cutting exercise it was. But there are many other examples, including the failure to deter Iraq in 1990. Moscow, too, has experienced the failure of deterrence, notably when Stalin became trapped by his own thinking and failed to deter Operation Barbarossa, and in 2008 when the Russian leadership assumed that the Russian forces deployed across the North Caucasus were enough to deter Georgia from launching military operations.[55]

A second problem is that since the end of the Cold War, the US and its allies have turned away from pursuing deterrence and towards a preference for preventative war. For some, therefore, deterrence has become a euphemism in lieu of a policy, a rhetorical device, rather than an element of a complex larger strategy to mitigate the risk of war. Deterrence is seen to 'cut across the grain' of traditional US military thinking, and few US defence planners subscribe to deterrence theory, preferring superiority and overmatch of opponents, and pre-emptive strikes in the name of defence – winning a war through striking first. If the invasion of Iraq in 2003 illustrated this approach, it was again illuminated by McMaster's statement in late 2017 when he observed, in relation to the emerging crisis with North Korea, that 'to accept and deter is not acceptable'. Thus some suggest that for the US defence community deterrence is no longer a general strategy for achieving national security or meeting alliance commitments, 'merely a set of activities that occur as part of preparation for war'. 'The central idea is no longer deterrence, but war', and deterrence is treated as 'making one's war preparation sufficiently visible to the enemy to encourage a painless surrender'.[56]

A third problem is that NATO allies have differing interpretations of the lexicon of deterrence, partly as a result of geography and partly as a result of capability, which engenders differences in the formulation of policy and strategy. These differing interpretations are based on the twin balance between central (or homeland) and extended deterrence (extending it to a third party), and between deterrence by denial – the attempt to decrease the probability that an adversary will achieve their objective – and by punishment – the imposition of prohibitive costs.

This latter balance between denial and punishment is a particular feature of the debate about how to deal with Russia. Particularly in terms of dealing with the hybrid threat, denial is the best option. This can best be done as the result of good governance, enhanced resilience measures and security sector reforms, and the reliability and capacity of police forces and interior ministries to cope with such challenges as civil disturbances and 'Occupy'-type movements. It will also mean continuing counter-corruption and enhanced security and counter-intelligence measures.[57] In this sense, these are not so much deterrence policies as outcomes in their own right with a deterrent effect.

In defence terms, North-Eastern Europe – the Baltic states in particular – is the main focus of the debate about whether Russia can be deterred by denial. Polish officials, for instance, are among those who advocate new NATO permanent bases and large troop deployments to deter Russia. This argument finds an echo in the US, where one influential study that explored the 'shape and probable outcome of a near-term Russian invasion of the Baltic states using conventional forces' asserted that such an invasion could not be successfully resisted – and thus advocated for a substantial increase to a force of seven brigades, of which three would be heavy armoured brigades adequately supported by airpower, land-based fire and other enablers to reinforce deterrence. The authors noted that while such an attack may not be likely, Moscow's recent behaviour suggests that NATO 'should take the prospect sufficiently seriously to

at least evaluate the requirements for deterring and, if necessary, defeating Russian adventurism'.[58]

The results of the war games were, the authors stated,
'unambiguous: as currently postured, NATO cannot successfully defend the territory of its most exposed members
... the longest it has taken Russian forces to reach the
outskirts of the Estonian and/or Latvian capitals of Tallinn
and Riga, respectively, is 60 hours'. 'Such a rapid defeat
would leave NATO with a limited number of options, all
bad', they continued, including a 'bloody counter-offensive,
fraught with escalatory risk, to liberate the Baltics, to escalate itself, as it threatened to do to avert defeat during the
Cold War, or to concede at least temporary defeat, with
uncertain but predictably disastrous consequences for the
Alliance, and ... the people of the Baltics'.[59]

This argument has merit – denial is widely considered
the best form of deterrence. And it reflects much of the
activity that the Euro-Atlantic community has begun to
implement since the Wales summit. But though it is a seduc-
tive argument, it is not the whole picture. There are three
main counter-arguments. First, it is an opening gambit for
a debate about ever-greater resources and a larger US presence in the region, a 'haggling exercise' over how many
US brigades should be deployed to Europe and where they
are placed, according to Kofman.

Second, Kofman also points out that creating robust
deterrence in the Baltic region is based on a misreading
of Russian military thinking, and instead of strengthening deterrence, it opens up a dual problem. On the one
hand, he notes, building a reinforced deterrent capability
risks escalating a security dilemma, leading to a Russian
response, in terms of either force repositioning (leading
to a net security loss for NATO and the states in the
region) or more aggressive behaviour in the region (effectively therefore creating a security paradox). On the other,
even quite substantial forward deployed forces in NATO's
'Army of Deterrence', he argues, would become hostage to
a Russian approach that, rather than attempting to invade

and occupy the Baltic states – by no means an easy task – would instead link up with Russian forces in Kaliningrad through Belarus. US forces would then be cut off within the range of powerful Russian missile systems, artillery and air attack. He provocatively – but emphatically – calls this the 'Battle of Dunkirk 2.0', and suggests that such reinforcement would not change the outcome of any such battle, but would simply 'lose the same battle but with more casualties'.[60]

Others, too, point out the problems inherent in deterrence by denial through forward basing. Retired US Air Force General Ralph Clem also notes NATO's imperative to reassure the Baltic states and deter Russia – but that assessments of the respective orders of battle and military geography make the Baltic states undefendable against a determined Russian attack in the early stages of a war. Clem argues that rather than basing increased US airpower in the Baltic states, where it would be exposed to Russian capabilities and so 'almost certainly be destroyed in the opening hours' of the war, there should be an effort to develop greater capacity to operate from bases in the UK, Western Germany, Denmark and the Netherlands.[61] Kofman and Clem both advocate a blend of deterrence, therefore – including denial, but also emphasizing deterrence by punishment through the ability to escalate a conflict both horizontally and vertically, and with superiority in sustainment.

Understanding 'The Other'

An essential element of shaping an effective deterrence posture is a more sophisticated understanding of Russian concepts and capabilities. Though the orthodoxy in the Euro-Atlantic community points to Russian aggression, the view from Moscow is rather different. Russian official documentation and speeches, combined with expert analysis, reveal concern about China's rise, instability in Central Asia, and a threat from an expansive Euro-Atlantic community that not only has overwhelming superiority over

Russia in terms of numbers, resources and technology, but has a 'proclivity for seeking regime change'.[62]

More broadly, officials point to increasing global instability, a 'sharp increase in the likelihood of a whole set of violent conflicts with either direct or indirect participation by the world's major superpowers'. Gerasimov has stated that in conditions of increasing competition over energy, labour resources and markets in which to sell their goods, some 'powers will actively use their military potential' and Russia may face military conflict on its own territory or in its neighbourhood. He noted that 'the spectrum of reasons and justifications for using military force is widening, and is all the more often being used to secure the economic interests of states under the slogan of defending democracy or promoting democratic values'.[63]

There is also much discussion of an international arms race. Putin has often pointed to this, notably in his Munich 2007 speech and in his 2018 interview on US TV Channel NBC, when he noted that this arms race began in 2002.[64] These points have underpinned a major decade-long effort to modernize Russian defence and security capabilities, enhance the coordination and resilience of the state, understand the changing character of war and work towards 'increasing the effectiveness of deterrence'.[65]

This has important implications for understanding and dealing with Moscow. Since the early 2010s, Russia has been a state in mobilization, moving onto a war footing and emphasizing defence and security readiness. This also has implications for the debate about deterrence by denial or punishment, and underlines the need for clear messaging. This will mean grasping Russian concepts of deterrence, and the differences between *sderzhivanie* – restraining a possible aggressor – and *ustrasheniye* – connoting offensive intimidation, and the perennial Russian concern about being surprised.

The primary feature of the Russian strategic debate is about strategic stability. This is at the heart of the 'different time zones' that the Euro-Atlantic community and Russia inhabit. For Moscow, contemporary security concerns are rooted in the past – influenced partly by Operation Desert Storm and NATO's Kosovo campaign. All the more influential, however, were the US withdrawal from the ABM Treaty in 2002, which Moscow saw as one of the foundations of strategic stability and US–Russia relations, and the invasion of Iraq in 2003, which Moscow denounced as illegal. On this basis, the Russian leadership has long and often stressed its objections to BMD and the Prompt Global Strike Programme. As Gerasimov noted in his 2013 article,

> already in 1991 the US military realised the concept of 'global sweep, global power' and 'air–ground' operations … now the concepts of 'global strike' and 'global missile defence' have been worked out, which foresee the defeat of enemy objects and forces in a matter of hours from almost any point on the globe while at the same time ensuring the prevention of unacceptable harm from an enemy counterstrike.[66]

Indeed, this combination has been at the heart of Russian strategic thinking ever since, a regular feature of Putin's highest-profile speeches about international affairs. It formed a significant part of his Federal Assembly speech in 2018, for instance, when he announced Russia's 'newest systems of Russian strategic weapons that we are creating in response to the unilateral withdrawal of the US from the ABM Treaty and the practical deployment of their missile defence systems both in the US and beyond their national borders'.[67]

These practical and conceptual processes mean that any Euro-Atlantic deterrence posture will need to understand the trajectory of how Russian capabilities and thinking are evolving. Deterrence, particularly in terms of denial, must avoid the hybrid bias and be forward looking. While there is no doubt that the Russian defence establishment recognizes the important role of non-military means in conflict, it is also very clear that alongside this, there is much reflection on the role of armed force. As Gerasimov has noted, the Russian armed forces must be ready to 'protect the state's interests in a military conflict of any scale with an adversary's extensive employment of both traditional and hybrid methods of confrontation. All the requisite decisions on increasing the combat capabilities of the army and navy have been taken and are being implemented.'[68]

If information is an important element of conflict, therefore, so is firepower, and the process of modernization of the equipment of the armed forces is ongoing, with an extensive shopping list of hardware from intercontinental missiles to aircraft and helicopters, 'muscular', well-armed ships, and thousands of tanks, armoured vehicles and self-propelled howitzers. Senior officials, including Putin and Gerasimov, have all emphasized the importance of the combat experience in Syria. Defence Minister Sergei Shoigu has stated, of the experience in Syria, 'for the first time in twenty-five years, Russian forces practically resolved the task of creating and using a powerful strike aviation group'.[69]

This means two things. First, there is a need for a detailed knowledge of the Russian defence industry and State Armaments Programme (GPV), and the nature, scale and sustainability of Russian arms procurement. Under GPV-2020, the progressive modernization of equipment is well under way, with a projected target of 70 per cent of equipment modernized by 2020. Once these targets are met, GPV-2027 signals a shift in focus from this intense process of renewal of weaponry to a more normal process of annual renewal.[70]

As important, however, is the second point: understanding how the Russian armed forces are learning and incorporating experience in the conduct of contemporary warfare, and how they think about future war. There is a rich educational environment: it incorporates not only the experience of the thousands of exercises the Russian armed forces have conducted themselves, and the campaigns in Ukraine and Syria, but also that of other wars and fighting, in Yemen, Nagorno-Karabakh, Iraq, Yugoslavia, Afghanistan, Gaza, Libya and Syria. The particular complexity here for Euro-Atlantic observers will be in understanding how those lessons take shape, and how they are grafted onto Russian military theory and history. Analysts should not be surprised when prominent Russian figures, including Gerasimov himself, can simultaneously discuss and weave together post-Cold War US activity, the war in Ukraine and lessons from the Soviet experiences of the 1930s and World War II, as they shape their understanding of the changing character of war and its contemporary and future characteristics.[71] As elsewhere, there are problems in Russia with both the procurement and lesson-learning processes. But without a clear focus on the modernization of equipment and the conceptual evolution of the changing character of war in Moscow, Euro-Atlantic thinking about Russian capabilities will be systematically and persistently obsolete.

The Challenges of Dialogue and Deterrence

The call for dialogue is still heard, mostly at presidential level. In May 2018, President Macron of France emphasized his desire to establish 'historic and strategic dialogue' with Putin, to 'align Russia with Europe and not to allow Russia to retire into itself'.[72] Similarly, Jean-Claude Juncker stated that he thought that Russia-bashing 'has to stop': 'we have to reconnect with Russia … to come back to, I would not say normal relations with Russia, but there are so many areas, so many domains, where we can cooperate'.[73]

Trump and Putin have held several telephone conversations. In December 2017, Putin spoke to Trump to thank him for the CIA's warning about a planned terrorist attack in St Petersburg – and promised reciprocity in the event of Russian services receiving information concerning terrorist threats to the US. In February 2018, they discussed the Middle East peace process. And the two presidents met in Helsinki in July 2018. But all told, the prospects for a substantial resuscitation of relations between the Euro-Atlantic community (particularly Washington and London) and Russia, are, in the short-to-medium term, limited and problematic.

That the meeting in Helsinki took place – and the way it was handled – caused a furore in the US, and concern among US allies. It also coincided with the US authorities announcing indictments of twelve Russian intelligence officers in connection with interference in the US elections, and was swiftly followed by the State Department further expanding sanctions against Russia over the attempted murder of the Skripals, and the drafting of a bill entitled the Defending American Security from Kremlin Aggression Act (DASKAA). In response, the Russian prime minister repeated the warning that any sanctions targeting Russian banking operations and currency trade would be seen as a declaration of economic war, and responded to by any means necessary.

Clearly, no form of 'engagement' or dialogue will be easy. The lack of trust is all too obvious: if politicians in the Euro-Atlantic community regularly accuse Moscow of lying, Russian officials and politicians reciprocate in equally vivid terms. When asked in late 2017 what political mistakes Russia had made in its relations over the past fifteen years, Putin instantly replied that 'our most serious mistake in relations with the West is that we trusted you too much. And your mistake is that you took that trust as weakness and abused it.'[74]

In any case, the Euro-Atlantic community has suspended high-level and practical dialogue twice in four years – first in 2014 with the war in Ukraine, and then again in 2018 following events in Salisbury. Though the Russian leadership has stated its readiness to resume dialogue, it should not be assumed that Moscow will simply accept Euro-Atlantic proposals, requests or negotiating points. And while Japan's eight-point plan offers a model for interesting possible areas for cooperation, it also illustrates that economic cooperation does not necessarily go hand in hand with political reconciliation, especially on core questions and if that 'reconciliation' means Moscow abandoning positions that the Euro-Atlantic community does not like.

Two points stand out, therefore, regarding 'engagement' with Russia. First, the phrase 'back to business as usual' is redundant and requires retirement – neither Brussels, nor Washington, DC, nor London should wish to 'return' to such a stagnant relationship. Moscow clearly has no intention of so doing. The focus will have to be on the future. Nevertheless, the forging of any new cooperative agenda will have to be done on the ruins of several previous attempts to build partnership. And some form of coexistence through a formula for disagreement and crisis management is more likely than any grand bargain'. Even in the important area of deconfliction and military-to-military contacts, this remains narrow and localized to specific issues relating to terrorism and Syria.

Second, there appears to be little appetite in Washington, London or Moscow to reach a settlement or to soften their posture. If achieving a settlement on Ukraine seems unrealistic, there seems to be little desire to attempt to settle the range of other questions. As one well-placed official in Washington stated in May 2018, after Georgia, Crimea, Eastern Ukraine, Syria, election interference, the 'NotPetya' cyber attack and Salisbury, amongst the other problems, there could be 'no wiping the slate clean and starting again'.[75]

Even when cooperation is portrayed as desirable, officials on both sides emphasize this should only be on their own terms, in their national interests. This approach has been obvious already for some time as senior politicians and officials have rhetorically held open their own door for cooperation, waiting for the other to accept the invitation and walk through it. But concessions from either side, let alone an acceptance of the other's positions, seem highly unlikely. Moscow, for instance, has made no serious concessions to Euro-Atlantic demands since the outbreak of war in Ukraine, and, as Director General of the Russian International Affairs Council Andrei Kortunov has noted, the way US policy is taking shape leaves Moscow little room for compromise:

if Vladimir Putin makes slight concessions on Syria, he'll be asked to abandon his partnership with Iran. If he is more flexible on Donbas, the issue of Crimea will be raised ... And we all know that Putin doesn't like to cave under pressure – be it foreign or domestic. So, there is no chance for some lasting compromise – at least one recalling the détente of the 1970s – even in the medium term.[76]

Any first step, therefore, will be to seek an easing of tension and finding a way of coexisting, or what British author Edward Crankshaw called 'putting up with' each other.[77] The accent, even for those who advocate a mixed approach combining dialogue and deterrence, is on deterrence. The Euro-Atlantic community, particularly in the shape of NATO, has not lost the ability to deter Russia – as illustrated by the lack of an armed attack on NATO (despite the pushing and shoving of power politics). Of course, it might also be said that this reveals one of the ambiguities of deterrence: how can we be sure that deterrence is succeeding in deterring something that has not happened? If there was no Russian plan to conduct an armed invasion of the Baltic states, then Russia has not been deterred from doing so.

Nevertheless, deterrence is no panacea, and indeed poses four further points for attention. First, the narrative of a shift from 'reassurance' to 'deterrence' to 'defence' suggests a conceptual conflation of terminology, one that facilitates the relabelling, retrofitting or repackaging of activity for convenience rather than adapting activity to meet requirements. This neither reassures allies, nor deters Russia. Care needs to be taken, therefore, that 'deterrence' does not become simply a box-ticking exercise – and that all the different activity that is under way does not become too overlapping, reliant on the same resources. It is also important to distinguish clearly between the various terms that are being used in this debate about deterrence: reassurance, tolerance, deterrence, provocation, coercion and contesting.

Related to this, second, questions remain over the aims and scope of deterrence. Should deterrence be extended beyond the alliance? Should the Euro-Atlantic community attempt to deter an escalation of the war in Ukraine? Or, as one US official put it, deter 'anything Moscow does that we do not like'? If Russian core interests in Ukraine outweigh those of the Euro-Atlantic community, this suggests that such deterrence would not succeed.[78] Similarly, if 'deterrence' is actually a broad term for seeking to prevent all kinds of Russian behaviour – such as 'obstructionism', 'malfeasance' or 'malign activity' and even domestic issues such as corruption and human rights abuses – but is additionally blurred with *punishment* (thus becoming the 'need to deter and to punish Russia', as one US official put it), this loses coherence and may lead to an escalation of tension.

This underlines the essential point that deterrence is difficult and can fail. This places emphasis on communication and misunderstanding – deterrence being a form of dialogue – and highlights the importance of effective strategic communications. But it is also the case that communications are beset by problems of interpretation: too often signals – even in plain language – from Moscow are not received in Euro-Atlantic capitals, let alone the more implicit signals the Russian leadership emits. Indeed, it often seems that beyond a small group of subject matter specialists, there is little awareness of what is being said in Russia about the US, the UK and NATO, let alone about how Euro-Atlantic deterrence is understood in Russia or how Russian deterrence is evolving. According to one NATO official, deterrence 'absolutely relies on understanding the adversary, but we do not understand Russian thinking, and we do not allow ourselves to consider that we do not understand it'.[79] At the same time, Washington, London and Brussels emit many and varied signals to Moscow, some deliberate, but many often apparently oblivious to how they are received.

Third, related to this, if a blend of deterrence by denial, particularly for hybrid concerns, reinforced by punishment for military and defence matters, is the best mix, how this relates to Russia requires consideration. There is scope for understanding better, for instance, how escalation might be managed. What would off ramps or routes for de-escalating a crisis look like – and how could they convincingly be conveyed to Moscow? Also, how will the progressive modernization of UK and US armed forces into the 2020s affect Moscow's understanding of strategic stability – and with what response and consequences?

Finally, fourth, there is a need to develop a better understanding of Russian defence and security thinking, Moscow's wider doubts and difficulties and the evolving trajectory of Russian capabilities and practices. Deterrence is currently too focused on a static, localized view of Russia. For it to be effective, a more active and dynamic approach to how conflict might begin and why is necessary, as is reflection on what are the points of competition – or areas of miscalculation – that might ignite it. It will need to be multi-layered, too, or as Michaels has put it, 'simultaneous deterrence'. In other words, it will not be through the 'narrow lens of a single case of success or failure at any given time', but include numerous activities ongoing simultaneously across the world in different theatres, often 'using the same overstretched capabilities', to deter more than one threat from several actors and actions.[80] Effective deterrence will also be about conducting a dynamic dialogue with Moscow that evolves over time. Deterrence must be forward-looking, ahead to 2020 and beyond, to encompass the ongoing military modernization, and the Russian leadership incorporates lessons being learnt from exercises and campaigns. This more sophisticated understanding will contribute to a refined grasp not just of Russian readiness measures, development trajectories and concerns, but also of the prospects of miscalculation.

Any attempt to rekindle substantive dialogue will have to go through the stages of, first, easing of tensions, and then the early stages of rebuilding trust. The first steps in resuscitating dialogue might include visits from parliamentary committees, and from retired senior officials to speak at events such as the Moscow International Security Conference. Such visitors should not expect a warm welcome, but would be going both to transmit and to receive messages. Some consideration should also be given to the development of technical, practical cooperation as a means of relationship building. It will also require a substantive agenda, one that is aware of what has worked and why and what is realistic given the extensive nature of disagreements. It will be a long-term project, looking at various channels through a diversified diplomacy dealing with the Russian Ministry of Defence as well as the Ministry of Foreign Affairs, and also looking into the next generation of leaders in politics, government, foreign service and military. Deterrence, too, to be effective, must include a greater focus on clarifying priorities and a forward-looking trajectory. Neither dialogue nor deterrence is an end in itself. Success in both will be the consequence of a coherent broader strategy.

4

Dealing with the Russians: Pillars of a Twenty-First-Century Strategy

The Prussian military thinker Carl von Clausewitz advocated that the first of all strategic questions, and the most comprehensive – indeed the 'most far reaching act of judgment that the statesman and military commander have to make' – is to establish the 'kind of war on which they are embarking, neither mistaking it for, nor trying to turn it into something that is alien to its nature'. War, he argued, should 'never be thought of as something *autonomous*, but always as an *instrument of policy*', and 'wars must vary with the nature of their motives and of the situations which give rise to them'.[1]

The Euro-Atlantic community and Russia are not at war. But tension is so high as to make Clausewitz's sound advice relevant. This was emphasized by events in spring 2018: the clash in February 2018 between US forces and pro-Assad regime forces, leading to the deaths of a number of Russian citizens, and the strikes on Syria by the US, France and the UK in April, preceded by statements by a Russian official that missiles fired at Syria would be shot down and the launch sites targeted, and a tense period of deconfliction before the strikes took place.[2] These events reflect the point that relations as a whole have all the features of competition – clashing interests and policies, as well as explicitly different values, and even a sense of ideology returning. It is a common view, particularly in Washington, DC, London and Moscow, that relations are likely to remain adversarial for some time.

The new era is already well under way, and therefore the terms of the debate have shifted. The language of war has returned to Europe, and Russia – for all its ongoing problems – is talked of as a near-peer or even peer power, with the existential threat this could pose. There are ongoing ambivalences in the discussion: the hangover (and often implicit) sense that Putin's departure from office could by itself lead to improved relations, that the ongoing weaknesses of Russia's economy will oblige Moscow to introduce far-reaching liberal reforms and seek better relations with the Euro-Atlantic community, and that Russian economic and demographic issues mean it will simply disappear as a problem. Regardless, the statement by a senior British defence official in 2016 that 'Russia is a reality on the world scene and we cannot go on pretending it is not' is correct.[3]

The persistent debate since the mid-2000s about whether the Euro-Atlantic community and Russia are in a 'new Cold War' has not helped Euro-Atlantic leaders to understand or predict Russian actions. This is because there can be no 'return' to some past era in history or repetition of history, even if the situation appears superficially similar, and because contemporary relations pose a very different set of problems, with different causes, geography, technology, and financial and socio-economic conditions, to say nothing of the fundamentally different international context. Clausewitz's advice emphasizes the need to focus on the kind of relationship that is emerging and why and how a war might actually break out.

From the 'New Cold War' Trap to Strategy-Making in a Post-Iraq War World

Numerous attempts have been made to replace such a catchy phrase as the 'new Cold War' or 'Cold War 2.0', from a 'clash of Europes' to a 'phony War' or a 'Cool War', the last used by the UK's Secretary of Defence to describe how he saw Russia attacking the UK on multiple fronts.[4] While all of these have their advantages, each is problematic – the 'clash of Europes' is now too regionally focused, the 'phony war' carries too much historical baggage and suggests a certain inevitability of trajectory, and the 'Cool War', in title at least, leans the debate towards the hybrid bias, minimizing the very real 'hot' aspects of what is happening in Ukraine and Syria.

An alternative is 'grey war'. It is 'grey', Dominic Selwood, a British author, has argued, because it includes electronic destabilization, hacking and 'weaponising' sensitive data to cripple targeted infrastructure. It is, he suggests, indirect, unattributable, ambiguous, unacknowledged, without defined edges and lacking a clear purpose. And it is the 'inevitable successor to the set piece warfare of the 20th century whose rule books and international conventions on the laws of war have spurred states like Russia to focus their energies on developing skills and expertise outside and beyond in places where there are few or no rules'.[5] This has advantages, such as its emphasis on being a successor to the twentieth century – that what is happening is new, and that history is not repeating itself – and the role of modern technology. Nevertheless, there is too much focus on the indirect, unattributable and unacknowledged nature of 'grey war' – when often it is indeed attributable, explicitly acknowledged and with important direct elements.

One Russian observer has suggested that it is more accurately termed a 'toxic war'. Like Selwood, the Russian observer Oleg Barabanov argues that the differences between the current crisis and the second half of the twentieth century are many. Barabanov states that the current crisis is based on a different paradigm, and old Cold War stereotypes could lead to a misunderstanding of the situation, and consequently to misguided political decision-making. He notes that the key features of the toxic war are the demonization of the enemy (most notably through the use of the

Hitler comparison), the denial of the adversary's right to exist (making dialogue impossible), trolling instead of diplomacy (a new variable in Euro-Atlantic–Russian conflict), interference in an adversary's domestic politics on a far greater scale, and big war being not just possible but desirable, with a fundamental strategic instability becoming a rule in toxic war.[6] These are vivid terms, but this comes closest to offering a fresh epithet that draws together the main features of the current relationship and approaches of both sides.

Even so, relations are more usefully characterized as a 'security challenge'. Though it lacks the flair of the other terms, it places the relationship on a spectrum between a 'security dilemma' and a 'security paradox'. A security challenge is when the dilemma of threat interpretation is settled, and only the dilemma of response remains. If the dilemma of response is then handled in a confrontational way, there is a risk of spiralling levels of mutual hostility towards a security paradox, when those policies intended to promote security cause the opposite. For many, the dilemma of interpretation is indeed clearly resolved – Russia as returning to its traditional role of aggressive, expansive state – and it only remains to work out how to shape an effective response to this. Some policies are already under way, including eFP and the re-establishment of some military structures (US 2nd Fleet), and the nature of the rhetoric, the lack of trust, the responses to the wars in Ukraine and Syria (including what is tantamount to an economic war) that suggest a looming, even imminent shift to a security paradox. The mutual suspicion, and with it mutual deterrence and the emphasis on both sides on defence readiness, speak to this shift.

The point of reference for thinking about how to deal with the situations, however, should not be the Cold War, but the Iraq war and particularly the findings and impact of the UK's Chilcot Inquiry and Report. This – not the Cold War – is the reference point for thinking about how to deal with Moscow. Indeed, not only does it provide the correct context for contemporary policy-making (the changed international environment, the shifts that have taken place in defence and security thinking and capabilities, and the post-Iraq relationship between Euro-Atlantic governments and their sceptical, not to say cynical, publics), it also brings a certain harmony to the question of how to conceptualize dealing with the Russians.

The war in Iraq reflected part of a new calculus in Washington and London about the nature of the world as it supposedly entered a new era after the 9/11 terrorist attacks. It illustrated what can happen when the 'architects of policy operate without testing their own assumptions, move on the basis of unquestioned common sense, making choices that are less calculated than axiomatic'. Furthermore, as Porter has argued, policy-makers were in the grip of a series of assumptions about Western insecurity, Western power and the relationship between the UK and the US. 'None of these assumptions have gone away', and 'in that sense', he wrote in 2016, 'the past is not even the past'.[7] Many of the conditions in dealing with contemporary Russia are strikingly similar: the relationship with Russia is part of a new calculus in Washington and London about the nature of the world as it supposedly entered a new era of state challenge, and politicians and policy-makers appear to be in the grip of a series of assumptions about Western insecurity, and the role and nature of Western power.

Moreover, using the Iraq war as an analytical focal point helps to align the dissonant chronologies between the Euro-Atlantic community and Russia discussed in the introduction. The invasion of Iraq was a pivotal moment for both sides, albeit in different ways. In Moscow's understanding of post-Cold War international affairs, the period 2002–4 was marked for the Russian leadership not only by the US withdrawal from the ABM treaty but also by the US-led invasion of Iraq. Much of subsequent Russian foreign and security policy has emerged in the wake of these developments.

The Iraq war was one of the main causes of the Euro-Atlantic policy community's loss of confidence. The war has proved deeply transformative, and in many ways shapes the context in which decisions are being made about international affairs today. In the UK, the long-running Iraq inquiry led by Sir John Chilcot, and the subsequent report, have exercised significant influence on policy-making, addressing the whole of the national security community and having been signed up to by senior staff. The Chilcot Inquiry and Report serve as an important indicator of whether the UK government can learn lessons from its failures and hold those who fail to account. As Sir John noted at the outset of the inquiry, the lessons would help to ensure that if the UK faced similar situations in the future, 'the government of the day would be best equipped to respond to those situations in the most effective manner in the best interests of the country'.[8] It is now the right lens with which to examine current practice regarding Russia.[9]

The Chilcot Test

Four points stand out in the critique of the UK in Iraq as being relevant here, as a test case for how the Euro-Atlantic community approaches the question of interpretation and response. First, there was a failure to understand not just the social, economic, political and cultural factors on the ground in Iraq, but also the UK's own capabilities. Second, there was a failure to apply critical thinking, and, as a result, groupthink exercised a negative influence on policy-making, particularly how momentum built around a core narrative. This narrative dominated the debate, 'putting it onto rails', according to one official, shunning both critics and evidence that did not fit, and those who could provide critique were either not heard or in the wrong place. Third, there was weak foresight, with little thought how the conflict in Iraq would play out; and there was no 'Plan B'. Finally, the UK's strategic communications 'failed internationally, domestically, and in theatre'. All told, therefore, strategy making was weak and inflexible, with poor resource allocation, weak negotiation within the alliance, particularly in the assumption of similarity with the US and an over-estimation of influence on Washington, and poorly handled strategic communications.[10]

The proposed responses include a range of measures, such as greater professionalization in role and careers. Responses also sought to exploit knowledge better to 'map thinking onto the real world rather than a world we might prefer' and to introduce 'reasonable challenge'. This latter point, 'reasonable challenge', is intended to avoid and counter groupthink as policy is being developed. It seeks the creation of an environment in which the articulation of different ideas is both expected and accepted, to highlight and explore alternative options and 'real diversity of thought rather than shades of mainstream thinking'. This can be done by incorporating evidence from beyond the immediate organization, including from think tanks, academia and other sources. Indeed, the Ministry of Defence's response insists that it is 'not optional': it is the 'duty' of civil servants to 'invite and offer challenge in the interest of good decisions'.[11]

The current situation with Russia, therefore, can be thought of as a test case for the implementation of the Chilcot Report: do policy thinking and policy-making on Russia pass what might be called 'the Chilcot test'? The argument in this book suggests that so far there is limited success. Thinking about (and therefore policy towards) Russia across the Euro-Atlantic community is in many ways reactive, and much of it fails to understand the social, economic, political and cultural factors on the ground in Russia. Instead, as we have seen, there is a narrow, abstract and clichéd view of Russia.

This has driven a narrative about Russia that has been – with some honourable exceptions – impervious to 'reasonable challenge', illustrated by the repetitive nature of the debate and constant sense of surprise. The groupthink of the Russia narrative is exemplified by the persistence of

the discussion about 'Russian hybrid warfare'. Senior officials respond to challenges to this with the statement that
there is little point arguing against it, because 'that ship
has sailed'. Indeed, 'Russian hybrid warfare' has retained
influence long after the majority of the specialist Russia-
watching community rigorously and repeatedly debunked
it and the existence of any 'Gerasimov Doctrine'. Either
the subject matter specialist challenge was ignored or over-
ridden, or there is too great a separation between expertise
and policy-making and the debunking was not conducted
on the right policy frequency to be effective.

Nearly five years after the outbreak of war in Ukraine
and four after the very different intervention in the war
in Syria, therefore, sophisticated understanding of Russia
remains restricted to lagoons. At large, thinking is abstract,
out of date and inaccurate, and curiosity about Russia,
to say nothing of empathy, is missing, while important
sections of established Russia expertise – even within
the policy-making community – are largely ignored,
even as those without specialist knowledge make it up
from scratch.

Taken together, this has led to a misdiagnosis of the
nature of the challenge as well as its scale and trajectory.
There is no doubt that the relationship has become increasingly adversarial. But rather than conflict caused by Russian
expansionism, the heart of the problem is possible war as
caused by competition, a clash of interests, priorities and
policies, not only about Euro-Atlantic security but more
broadly about international affairs. This puts the debate
about 'dialogue' or 'deterrence' in a different light.

Treated as they are as separate approaches, dialogue
and deterrence reflect an attempt to manage the situation,
to deal with problems as they arise, rather than shape an
overall direction. But they are not goals in themselves:
each can only be effective as parts of a wider whole, and
both are the consequences of having a clear idea of what
is wanted from the relationship with Russia and how to
achieve it.

The Need for Grand Strategy for the New Era

The antidote to the roll of day-to-day events and friction that drives the ongoing deterioration in relations lies in shaping a coherent strategy that illuminates not only the path already travelled and where we are today, but also a path ahead, uniting things that work, and providing a track to building relations and a purpose to early meetings, as well as effective prioritization, interaction and signalling. It is also about understanding the consequences of policies advocated and implemented.

The fundamentals of strategy are easily sketched out: strategy is the relationship between ways, means and ends, or, more practically, the formulation of a coherent, adequately resourced agenda, and then its implementation. It is an executive process – setting an agenda and taking the initiative. This is not easy: strategy never is, as plans are buffeted by events, even before they can be implemented, and with the dynamic interaction between all the parties involved, at home and abroad, in a constantly changing environment. But shaping a strategy for dealing with Moscow will serve to place the relationship in the wider contemporary international context, move the debate on from twentieth-century rhetoric and guide more sophisticated thinking about Russia's role in international affairs. Indeed, there is little choice but to attempt to think strategically. Many states – and non-state actors – across the world, including in Europe and in the Middle East, as well as the US, China and Russia, are facing fundamental strategic questions at a time of international instability. As the British authors Paul Cornish and Kingsley Donaldson have written, 'only strategy in its fullest political-military sense will enable Western governments to manage the complexity and dynamism of the 21st century ecosystem in which they find themselves'.[12]

And many are advocating the need for such a strategy specifically regarding Russia. In the US, there have been many calls for a US grand strategy towards Russia, and papers setting out 'road maps' for US–Russia relations or advocating the need for a strategy of containment.[13] And the UK's House of Commons Foreign Affairs Committee stated in May 2018 that instead of reacting in an ad hoc and disjointed manner, 'the UK must set out a coherent and proactive strategy on Russia, led by the Foreign and Commonwealth Office and coordinated across the whole of government, that clearly links together the diplomatic, military and financial tools that the UK can use to counter Russian state aggression'.[14]

What might such a strategy look like? In Washington, there is an ongoing debate. Fiona Hill, for instance, prior to taking up a position on the US National Security Council, argued that a strategy for Russia could be based on four points: it would be realistic, in accepting that there are some concessions that either side will not make; it would build on incremental demands rather than a 'grand bargain', including persuading Moscow that there would be a benefit to changing its behaviour; it would be flexible, having the structure to deal with Russia over the long term; and it would be unified across NATO and the EU, with tailored outreach initiatives to individual states. This last point – unity – she considered to be the critical element in any strategy for dealing with Russia.[15] And Russia has begun to feature in Washington's strategic planning and documents.

But observers are cautious or critical in their assessment of Washington's strategy. High-profile figures such as McFaul assert that the US looks 'weak as never before' and the absence of a 'coherent, unified grand strategy for dealing with Russia makes it difficult to forge bipartisan support at home or allied abroad'.[16] First, there is an important ambiguity in how the US policy community sees Russia. Broadly put, this view of Russia oscillates in its assessment of Russia between its being the main threat to the US and a state in decline, whose GDP is equal to that of Portugal.

In this view, Russia is a competitor but one that does not require a great deal of investment because the threat it poses today will 'evaporate when Russia inevitably collapses under the weight of its economic, political and demographic contradictions'. It is time, therefore, to part with illusions about Russia, and to consider increasing spending across a wide range of tools of statecraft – though there is 'not much evidence of a national conversation about what would be required to undertake this approach', according to the US observer Nikolai Gvosdev.[17]

Others argue that the US response to Russia has been one with no positive agenda. Largely in the absence of other tools, and particularly since the shooting down of MH17 in 2014, the use of sanctions has been the defining feature of Washington's approach to US–Russia relations, but this approach has done little to alter Russian behaviour. Moreover, the sanctions have become less specifically tailored to Russian activity in Ukraine, instead looking towards a much wider range of activities defined as 'countering Russian influence in Europe and Eurasia', including human rights abuses.[18]

Much of this confusion is due to the nature of the debate about Russia. According to Eugene Rumer of the Carnegie Endowment, the US is in the throes of a 'national obsession' with Russia, one that 'prevents sane debate'. 'Our national conversation about Russia – what we want from the debate, how to achieve it – has barely advanced', he continued, and 'the more hysterical we get, the harder it will be for us to have that conversation'.[19] The same can be said for the debate in the UK.

Few seem to have any idea how to improve relations, and this approach, combined with Congress's efforts to constrain the Trump administration's ability to reverse that punishment, let alone improve relations, 'locks US–Russia relations into a path of confrontation and offers no off-ramp from rising tensions'.[20] Importantly, the allegations of collusion will make it difficult for the Trump administration to attempt to offer a new approach to improving relations with Russia, all the more so if there are further allegations of interference in the mid-term elections in 2018 or in 2020. John Huntsman, the US Ambassador to Russia, has already noted that relations would be 'done' if the Kremlin attempted to interfere in the 2018 midterms, but also that he did not 'think Russia is going to quit'.

Even in confrontation, however, questions are being posed of US strategy. According to some, the National Defense Strategy does not offer a strategy for coping with Russia. Instead, it has a 'retro, 1980s vibe', harking back to the competition that was, rather than the contemporary challenge. In any case, Kofman argues, the document is more of a recitation of grievances about classic power behaviour rather than an attempt to lay out a Russia strategy as the Pentagon understands it, or what the two countries are competing over and the differences between what the US simply does not like and what it seeks to contain. Moreover, the document fails to show how the US will cope with Russian strategy and seek to gain leverage, not least because it focuses on certain Russian capabilities rather than an understanding of how the adversary approaches the use of military and non-military instruments, their strategy and the nature of competition.

Finally, the document is limited in horizon – addressing grievances in scenario-based assessments largely confined to Russian behaviour in Europe. This returns us to the overall ambiguity of the Washington, DC, policy community's approach to Russia: all told, Kofman states, again the main thrust of the policy community's assumptions about Russia are that it will 'go away some time in the 2020s', either because it will run out of money or people, or because it will 'spontaneously turn into a democracy with no conflicting national interests'. There is a 'hidden assumption that Russia will depart the scene and allow the Pentagon to have the more intimate competition with China that it so very much desires'.[21]

In London, there also appears to be some ambiguity in shaping a strategy for dealing with Russia. This is partly because of Russia's important but somewhat ambivalent place in UK priorities. While senior politicians and officials assert that Russia is a major priority for London, other important matters jostle for attention, most notably Brexit, but also the US–UK 'special relationship', as well as a wide range of other pressing questions, including China's role in international affairs, climate change and migration, and domestic questions. International terrorism and the now diminished but lingering threat posed by Daesh also continue to pose a major question for the UK. In early June 2018, newly appointed Home Secretary Sajid Javid unveiled a new counter-terrorism strategy to cope with what he called one of the 'starkest threats' the UK faces, and the UK's security service emphasizes the threat posed by terrorism as being 'intense, unrelenting and multidimensional'.[22] All of this dilutes the ability to focus on Russia.

Second, since the attack in Salisbury in March 2018, the UK has sought to strengthen, even lead, an anti-Russia alliance, using four major summits (the G7, the G20, NATO and the EU) in 2018 to 'call for a comprehensive strategy to combat Russian disinformation and urge a rethink over traditional diplomatic dialogue with Moscow', as well as calling for a new rapid response unit to counter Russian 'malfeasance', including cyber attacks and assassination attempts.[23] But despite occasional interventions in 2014, when the British government, then led by David Cameron, lobbied the EU to impose sanctions on Russia (alongside measures to support Ukraine), for well over a decade London has been content to take a less direct role in dealing with Russia, with the focus being on how to engage the US on the Russia question, or by supporting German leadership of Europe's relationship with Russia.

London has not been a primary point of contact between the Euro-Atlantic community and Russia, therefore, and the UK is not party to some of the main discussion formats with Moscow, such as the Normandy or Minsk Groups. Cameron, for instance, did not believe he could play a brokering role similar to that which then French President

Sarkozy had played in 2008, particularly without US support. Thus Cameron took 'a back seat' in relations with Moscow, supportive of Berlin's leadership and 'even content to go along with the perception that France is a pivotal ally working with Germany trying to resolve Ukraine ... but jibes that Britain is absent from the top table hurt'. This indirect approach to Russia was part of a broader foreign policy that was widely criticized for representing the UK's retreat from international affairs.[24]

Towards a Strategy?

A British strategy for dealing with Russia can be traced to the January 2015 meeting of the National Security Council,[25] and it has been evolving since then. The basis of the strategy can be detected in what might be called a 'four pillars plus' formula – four main pillars plus a series of other documents and speeches that both add further colour and capture the evolution and development since then. Broadly, the four pillars are: to protect UK interests and those of its allies (effectively, deterrence); to engage Russia in global security issues and other areas of shared interest; to promote the UK's values, including those of a rules-based system; and to build stronger links between the British and Russian peoples, developing people-to-people contacts and civil society.[26]

Other relevant indications include then Defence Secretary Michael Fallon's speech in February 2017, during which he stated that British priorities, based on a 'clear eyed assessment of Russian behaviour', would be to increase coordination in NATO and the EU, to 'counter Putin's pravda' and to reinforce deterrence. The UK had sought partnership, he argued, but Moscow had 'chosen competition', and thus the UK would 'engage but beware', in the hope that Moscow would 'abide by Minsk, curb the reckless military activity and ditch the misinformation'. If Moscow did so, there was the 'potential for better relations' and it could once 'again become the partner the West always wished for'.[27]

And speaking in November 2017, Theresa May emphasized the UK's commitment to the rules-based order 'against irresponsible states that seek to erode it', and to strengthening the commitment, purpose and unity of allies and partners with whom the UK has built this order. The UK, she noted, is 'unconditionally committed to maintaining European security'. Her 'very simple message' for Russia was 'we know what you are doing and you will not succeed. The UK will do what is necessary to protect ourselves and our allies.' This included the reform of NATO, deterring and countering hostile Russian activity, and increasing military and economic support to Ukraine, strengthening the UK's cyber security and tightening financial regimes. At the same time, she reiterated the point Fallon had made about the UK's posture of 'beware but engage'.[28]

There is much activity under way on these objectives and it has taken on a more cross-government character since spring 2018. As noted, the UK seeks to lead a multinational alliance to address the Russian challenge, and London has spent considerable effort contributing to NATO's eFP and other collective defence measures, and attempting to consolidate the UK's own security.

At the same time, there are problems. In the wake of Iraq particularly, and despite some improvements, British strategy-making writ large has been persistently critiqued for the difficulties it has faced translating innovation into a coherent national security agenda, maintaining institutional coordination across government, sustaining and consolidating civil service expertise and experience, and articulating national security policy to a general public that is sceptical of government and the use of force.[29] Much of this relates more specifically to the UK's Russia strategy.

Second, statements by senior British figures, including both May and Fallon, emphasized that the UK was *responding* to Russian actions (real and perceived), and urged

Moscow to change course. As May said, many in the UK had 'looked at post-Soviet Russia with hope' that it would 'one day choose a different path of responsibility in promoting international stability'. 'Russia can, and I hope one day will, choose this different path', she stated, 'but for as long as Russia does not, we will act together to protect our interests and the international order on which they depend.' This seems too passive, and to leave the initiative to Moscow, rather than offering a guiding initiative for the UK's own interests.

Furthermore, while there is much activity, this could be better coordinated both internally, to ensure efficient use of resources, and externally, to ensure coherent signalling to the Russian leadership. There are also gaps between the demands of politics and the rigours of policy, and between the shorter-term focus of policy and longer-term strategy. In addition, there is a strong sense of a persistently external and geographically partial view of Russia and how it works. Too much emphasis is placed on the coherence of Moscow's activity, even the assumption of a 'seamless conduct of policy' and its ability to seize opportunities on the international stage, even though there is a great deal of evidence to the contrary. And much of the UK's attention to Russian activity also appears to be focused on European developments, which, while undoubtedly important, is an approach that is too narrow.

Finally, the signalling of the strategy could be improved. On the one hand, there is too little outreach to the British population to persuade them of the value of the UK's strategy. While it is referred to in various documents and speeches by senior figures, it is often implicit, not very clearly articulated or revealed only in a quickly forgotten speech. As a result, civil servants often find themselves challenged about its existence. This need not breach valid security concerns: though a document does not a strategy make, even a relatively simple statement outlining context, purpose, resources and goals made available on appropriate government websites would be an improvement.

On the other, it is not clear that signalling to Moscow is satisfactory. Senior political figures quoting Voland from Bulgakov's *The Master and Margarita* may transmit unexpected and unintended messages to Russian audiences, while statements such as those urging Russia to change 'tack, abide by Minsk, curb the reckless military activity and ditch the misinformation. If it does then there is the potential for a better relationship' and Russia 'could again become the partner the West always wished for' may appear to a Russian audience as 'Russia should change, Russia will change' and a rather bald demand to surrender.[30] This may feel good to a British politician, but it will receive short shrift in Moscow. And this assumes, of course, that the narrative is focused primarily on Russia and the Russian leadership: some of the statements by senior British officials have appeared to be more focused on other parts of the UK government, particularly the Treasury in a budget bid. This was even noted by some Russian observers in the wake of speeches by senior British military personnel in early 2018.

And, finally, to quote Churchill, however beautiful the strategy, one should occasionally look at the results. If there are pillars and documents that frame a British strategy towards Russia, and attempts to make it a whole-of-government strategy, it is not clear that that strategy is yet working. Relations continue to deteriorate, concerns run high – or are increasing – about the Russian threat to the UK and its allies, the promotion of British values with regard to Russia does not show great success, and engagement of any form is truncated.

Nevertheless, a strategy is a process, and will take time to show significant results. In this case, the important events in spring 2018, both in terms of relations with Russia and for UK and Euro-Atlantic strategy-making, offer an opportunity to review it and reflect what else can be done. On the basis of the 'Chilcot test', two more pillars could be beneficially added to the UK's strategy. Both of these pillars relate to the conceptualization and formulation elements of strategy; implementation can be subsequently developed.

The Fifth Pillar: Challenging Groupthink

The fifth pillar relates to developing better thinking about Russia. As the House of Commons Defence Committee stated in 2016, 'of primary importance is the need for greater understanding as the basis for a more informed strategy and for better communications to avoid unintended escalation to open conflict'. 'We cannot hope to respond militarily to Russia without first understanding its way of thinking: this cannot be achieved without communications and dialogue.'[31] This must include 'reasonable challenge'.

This will mean a coherent, sustained and thorough reinvigoration of Russia expertise both in state structures and beyond, since a coherent and effective strategy will require a realistic and sophisticated understanding of the many aspects of Russia, including the Russian leadership's thinking, capabilities, strengths, weaknesses, doubts and difficulties. The limits of Russia expertise and the 'slow death' of Russia studies have been a recurring lament since the mid-2000s.[32] It is a theme that re-emerges and repeats every couple of years or so, most recently in late 2017 and spring 2018. Its centrality to 'understanding' and 'reasonable challenge' warrants a brief reiteration of the main points.

The principal point is that there is too little sophisticated expertise on Russia, because of a lack of funding and career opportunity, and that which does exist is overwhelmed by 'simplistic and misguided jingoism'. The consequences are that there are too few specialists and Russian-language speakers, answering too narrow a set of questions since the 1990s, especially questions of general foreign policy, democratization and the development of civil society and protest movements. As a result, Euro-Atlantic governments are frequently surprised by Russian activity, and their policies towards it are often ill-informed: as one former US

Treasury official suggested, the 'bottom line is that the US government has a very shallow bench on Russia. And so they end up acting more or less at random.'[33]

The US academic Tim Frye has argued against this, pointing out that Russia studies in political science is thriving, with innovative research and numerous articles being published in leading journals. Moreover, he emphasized the establishment of the University Consortium, a substantially funded project that brings together leading universities from the US, UK, Germany and Russia.[34] This is to be welcomed. But the consortium itself acknowledges that it is educating a new generation – this is a future-oriented programme. And while the publication of articles in leading journals is good news, the subjects largely reflect a continuation of a similar agenda to that which has dominated the last twenty years: democracy, leadership popularity and protest. Moreover, policy-makers tend not to read such publications. To be sure, these are important subjects and to be pursued – and there has been an explosion of work produced on the currently fashionable subjects of 'Russian hybrid warfare', information and media.

A Change of Focus

But if there is an ongoing debate about the need for a 'radical re-conceptualisation of relations with Russia' in terms of redressing the over-focus on Vladimir Putin and Russia's democratic shortcomings,[35] it is also the case that there are many different themes to pursue, requiring specialized knowledge. There is a need for a shift in big-picture assessment of Russia, therefore, but also for important technical detail. And with the opening of a new era of relations with Russia comes a different set of questions and the need for another set of skills. Indeed, the outbreak of war in Ukraine – emphasized by the war in Syria – struck at the very weakest, most limited part of Euro-Atlantic expertise on Russia: sophisticated and detailed knowledge about Russian military, intelligence and security thinking and capability. Indeed, the focus on the Gerasimov Doctrine emerged because of the limits of understanding of Russian military and security matters, and the capacity of the comparatively small community of specialists has often been absorbed in repeatedly debunking this, rather than sketching out a more sophisticated understanding. Related to this, there are shortfalls across a number of complex subjects, from Moscow's nuclear escalation decision-making to Russian space capabilities.

In Russian foreign policy, too, there are important gaps. While there are good generalists, there are very few specialists who combine the skills necessary to produce sophisticated research on increasingly relevant regional questions – Russo–Iranian relations, for instance, Russian policies in the Gulf or Russo–Turkish relations. Even the strategically important Russo–Chinese relations remain the remit of a very few genuine specialists with access to the necessary sources in both Russia and China. And there is a shortage of expertise in understanding how the Russian economy works and the wider Russian socio-economic sector – from defence economics to agriculture, pharmaceuticals and the health sector, from artificial intelligence to climate change, and from Russian infrastructure to urbanization. Even in the energy sector, there is a limited understanding of the scope and scale of the activities of Rosneft, Gazprom and Rosatom.

The Russia studies community of course has much to offer to the academic, public and public policy discussion. But since the end of the Cold War it has become largely separated from the wider, mainstream strategic studies and policy debate. Not only is a refocus on a wider range of questions necessary, therefore, but so is a re-engagement with other research communities. A much more multidisciplinary approach is required, reaching across debates both to contribute to and, importantly, to draw more on economics, sociology, history, international relations and strategic studies. The requirements of learning about the Russian military, space activity, urbanization or infrastructure will mean much greater familiarization with the often complex

technical and theoretical aspects of those fields. This also
means working with other area studies communities: productive cooperation between Russia watchers and Sinologists, for instance, or specialists on the Middle East and
North Africa, remains too rare.

Coordinating Knowledge

At the same time, a new balance between a reinvigorated
Russia studies community and state structures will need to
be struck. State structures in the US and UK are among
those attempting to rebuild their Russia expertise. Recognizing that the challenge will be 'with us for the next decade
and beyond', the UK launched the 'EECADRE' in 2015 to
recruit and retain a 'strong network of officials who develop
successful careers anchored' in the region and to build a
'deep understanding of the region ... to develop and deliver
first rate policy'.[36] They also acknowledge that this will
take time, and requires a long-term investment, but there
is already a significant increase in resources visible, in terms
of both numbers of individuals focused on Russia and state
resources. Similarly, in the US, the Russia Strategic Initiative provides the Department of Defense with the means
to analyse Russia-related issues across government, academia
and think tanks to generate a broader perspective. A shift
is already under way, therefore, in the structure of the
Russia-watching community, and state capacity in terms
of numbers is starting to outweigh independent academic
and think tank resources.

But ongoing shortfalls remain in language capabilities and in institutional memory of and knowledge about
Russia and relations with it, what has worked and what has
not and why, who is who and why, and how Russia works.
The reduction in numbers in embassies following the mutual
expulsions in spring 2018 underline this, for the time being,
at least. These are all areas where external researchers can
make a contribution. But the relationship between state
structures and independent research is not an easy one. Not

only do they speak very different professional languages, but approaches to the subject are very different – in the words of one senior civil servant, the two communities 'often live in competing ivory towers, each doing their own thing in ignorance of the other' – making communication difficult.

Equally, if the call, often repeated over the years by numerous parliamentary committees, for the government to reach out to academic research is the right one, this has not proved an easy balance to strike. As the authors of one report noted, government 'often struggles to draw on academia effectively in forming policy'. It is often caught, for example, between inefficient institutional arrangements and informal (and often rather transient) personal contacts. Contacts between academia and policy thus remain 'ad hoc, inconsistent and fragile'. This is because of divisions between departmental analysts and policy units, unclear responsibility for engagement with academia, little coordination across government and high staff turnover.[37]

It is not always easy to connect research usefully to policy. Not all academic work does or should relate to policy – particularly not the more theoretical and methodological aspects. And when it does, there is a dual problem. On the one hand, policy requirements are moving beyond the work that the majority of the Russia studies community is producing. On the other, some argue that those working in policy can feel that 'academic engagement is clumsy and naïve', of frustratingly poor quality, and ranging from 'jargon-laden "briefs" that contain little pertinent information to condescending homilies about what democratically elected politicians should care about'. As one observer has noted, therefore, 'for research truly to inform policy, it is not enough to hope that the stars will align. The stars need to be wrestled into position.' Nevertheless, recommendations that government funders should 'force universities to take policy impact seriously', and research-intensive universities should set up dedicated policy-impact units staffed by professionals who are adept at navigating academia and policy, are contentious.[38]

'Impact' is an important requirement for academia, and the search for policy relevance can have a significant impact on research agendas and funding – a good example being the 'hybrid war' phenomenon. This can have negative results, and a form of enhanced groupthink can take shape, with external, 'independent' work geared to what observers see to be the current policy concerns and thus serving to solidify or calcify government positions. It is not necessarily the case, therefore, that reaching beyond government circles will lead to 'reasonable challenge'.

Academic research should maintain an independent and curiosity-driven approach – academics should decide on individual research proposals, rather than politicians doing so. This does not mean that research cannot subsequently be put to policy ends, but it raises the question of 'whether the impact narrative should drive the research or vice versa'.[39] Failing to maintain intellectual independence and curiosity can too easily result in becoming a fig leaf of confirmation of government biases and entrench groupthink. Nevertheless, a primary benefit of better links between the public policy community and external, independent research will be first to maintain and then to enhance sophisticated reasonable challenge. This fifth pillar is essential for the sixth – shaping a strategy for Russia in the wider and longer-term context.

The Sixth Pillar: Russia in the Wider and Longer-Term Context

This pillar has a number of important features, including assessment of a more holistic view of Russia, how the Russian leadership views the UK, and the broader evolving context of international affairs, and particularly the places (and priorities) of Russia and the UK in it.

A More Holistic View of Russia

In May's November 2017 speech, Russia occupied an important place in the first part of her remarks, before she turned to treat separately other questions such as the Middle East and an agenda for 'Global Britain' – including global economic growth, partnership with Asia and Africa, and seeking out and securing new markets from the Gulf to East Asia. One of Britain's biggest assets, she concluded, is the UK's soft power, and the role of UK companies bringing good governance as well as commercial benefits.

But Russia cannot be treated separately from this 'Global Britain' agenda, since the UK will have to deal with Russia across all these geographic and thematic areas. The task of 'Global Britain', indeed, framed as defending the rules-based order, is part of a direct and explicit competition and evolution in the world order that Russia has long argued is under way and sees as being confirmed with each crisis.

Indeed, if the most obvious feature of the Euro-Atlantic discussion about Russia is its abstract nature, another is its compartmentalization, not to say fragmentation. Too often, 'Russia' features in thinking only as an Eastern appendage to Europe, Russian activity is seen in isolation, and relations with Russia in bilateral or geographically localized terms. Russian actions in Syria are too often treated separately from the situation in Ukraine, or the Arctic, for example, and activity in the Arctic, for instance, is too often seen in terms either of security *or* of energy, rather than as part of a more integrated whole of security *and* energy. This has led to a series of very partial and incomplete views and analyses of Russian activity.

A more holistic approach is necessary, one that includes a wider and better-coordinated picture of Russian geography, including Russian activity in the Asia-Pacific region, East Asia and beyond. An obvious illustration would be Russian defence and security measures: while the wars in Ukraine and Syria pose very different sets of questions for Moscow, they should be understood together in the light of the rebuilding of wider Russian defence and security capability. While Russia's Zapad exercises are an obvious point of focus for the Euro-Atlantic community, the other major strategic exercises – Vostok, Tsentr and Kavkaz – should be treated as equally important. Similarly, the way the Russian leadership has sought to coordinate its capabilities in major exercises illustrates not only how the military is being organized across different regions of the country, and moving forces great distances across Russia, but how defence is integrated with internal security measures and the activities of a wide range of state ministries and agencies. Thinking about Russian security should also therefore be extended, for instance, to include the roles of the Ministries of Health, Communications and Transport, as well as civilian regional authorities.

Equally important is the weaving together of economics and energy as essential aspects of Russian state security thinking, which also illustrate the importance of seeing Russian activity with a wider geographical lens. Russian security thinking, for instance, includes concerns not only about political and informational activity, but also about financial-economic measures and energy competition. There has been a shift in Moscow's thinking about the role that the economy plays in international conflict, and the Russian leadership considers the sanctions to be one of the instruments being used to contain Russia. As a result, Richard Connolly argues, Russian economic policy is being subordinated to 'concerns of a broader national security'.

Similarly, as the specialist in energy security and geopolitics Nazrin Mehdiyeva points out, the Russian leadership sees energy exports to be the key factor in Russia's economic development and Russia's place in international economic and political affairs. A threat to energy exports through competition is a threat to the budget, and so a national security matter. Thus, 'spurred by the sanctions, deprived of access to technology and finance and fearful of the loss of energy markets and influence', Moscow is enhancing its relationships in Asia, particularly with China.[40]

If the government is attempting to rebuild its Russia expertise, there is also the need to ensure that this expertise works efficiently together to ensure that information and analysis is coherently passed across the correct departments. This suggests the need for better coordination of existing knowledge within government structures, across ministries and departments. It too often seems that existing knowledge in one part of government is not well shared with others, meaning that it has been doubled up or had to be relearnt. Given the importance of how geographical regions link together, for instance, those dealing with security and defence could be better coordinated with those dealing with energy, and connecting across regions.

Moscow's Views of the UK

Second, to echo Marc Bloch again, the adversary is a constant headache for the strategist. Having a sophisticated view of how Moscow sees the UK and where the UK fits in Russian strategic thinking should be a feature of any UK Russia strategy, because it will indicate the parameters of what is possible. This is important because while UK policy-makers and politicians may assume that Moscow 'must understand' the UK and its actions, the Russian leadership is as vulnerable to mirror-imaging, cognitive dissonance, confirmation bias and misunderstanding as Euro-Atlantic governments. Furthermore, it will clarify the point that specific actions or policies by the UK – or the wider Euro-Atlantic community – will not necessarily significantly change Russia's *overall* trajectory, because much of Moscow's strategic agenda is guided by what the Russian leadership sees as essential modernization processes or a wider context of international competition. It is unlikely that London – or Washington or Brussels – will be able to convince Moscow to not pursue policies that it sees as essential to Russian national security.

If the limits to UK expertise on Russia are recognized, therefore, it is worth asking what the state of Russian expertise on the UK is, both in government and beyond. Though there are some pockets of experienced, specialist knowledge, most Russian attention is focused on other priorities, particularly the US, with the UK featuring as only of tangential or passing interest. Thus, while there is some visible research on specific technical aspects of the UK – such as military capability – which should not be underestimated, there is a mixed picture and it is open to question how well coordinated this expertise is and what impact it has on state policy.[41]

And if many in the UK find the British decision-making and policy-shaping process characterized by opacity, not to say disorder, and marked by 'incoherence, variation, informality and individuality',[42] to what extent can Russian observers be expected to grasp the finer details? To what extent are Russian officials and observers able accurately to decipher UK signalling? If it is a commonplace, albeit a misleading one, in the Euro-Atlantic discussion that the Russian leadership is unpredictable, are UK politics or policy-making any more predicable to Moscow? And what implications does this have for deterrence?

This will also mean posing a series of questions that may be sensitive, since realistic answers will not be welcome news. In broad terms, for instance, Moscow's consistent position over the last decade has been that Anglo-Saxon influence and power in international affairs are in strategic, long-term decline. Does Moscow consider the UK to be Russia's peer or even a near-peer, both in specific domains and overall? What is Moscow's understanding of the UK's planned Joint Force 2025, a plan to double its expeditionary force to 50,000 personnel, a maritime task group built around a new aircraft carrier, a land division with three brigades, as well as air and special forces groups?[43] Again, either in terms of Moscow's disagreements over Euro-Atlantic expeditionary wars, or in how it is seen as a feature of an emergent arms race, what does this mean for future deterrence?

The UK is often prominent (and subject to much vitriolic comment) in the Russian media, including by senior politicians and officials. A prominent Russian observer even noted the emergence of the theory that the UK has been Russia's main geopolitical opponent over the past 300 years.[44] Yet it has all but disappeared from explicit mention in formal Russian strategic thinking. In the 2013 Foreign Policy Concept, the UK was noted broadly alongside Germany, France, Italy and the Netherlands, as the document stated that Russia would like the potential of interaction with the UK to be used for the development of mutually beneficial relations, for putting the Russian 'economy on the innovative development track'.[45] But there was no mention of the UK in the 2016 version of the Concept.

Informally, Russian officials have suggested that London is not a priority for Moscow, particularly compared to Washington and Berlin. Indeed, relations were so poor by 2016 that the UK's embassy in Moscow was seen as 'toxic', according to one Russian official, and London was not seen as an influential interlocutor. On the one hand, the most important relationship was with Washington, DC, and London was merely the US's junior partner that could be bypassed. On the other, London was seen as less likely to be able to offer any substantive dialogue or partnership than some European capitals.[46] London is seen not only as an awkward, critical interlocutor, but as a peripheral one. While Russian officials state that Moscow is ready to change its position at any time on terms acceptable to it, the implications of the decade-long, structural set of disagreements have meant that a deep-set negative atmosphere in Moscow should be the starting point for any UK strategy looking ahead.

Looking Ahead

This leads to the third feature. For a Russia strategy to be effective, it requires both a broad horizon, contextualizing Russian activity, and a realistic grasp of the various possible trajectories taking shape. This will need an understanding not only of the UK's own priorities and trajectory, but also of Moscow's priorities and intended trajectory, how the Russian leadership sees international affairs evolving and Russia's relations with other states, such as China, and where and how UK and Russian trajectories may interact over the next five to ten years. This would provide the flexible intellectual architecture for shaping a relationship over a decade, therefore, and guide resources to these ends. It would also help to shed light on bigger-picture questions of the roles not just of Russia, but also of China and India.

Clear and careful assessment of trajectories will help to clarify the ambiguity about whether Russia is 'in decline' or not and what that means for relations. Also, though for many in Washington (but also in other European capitals) there is no possibility of agreement with Putin, there are those who await his departure. Consideration of the 'post-Putin' period, whenever that may be, should form part of strategic ten-year outlook analysis.[47] But this is not an argument for calibrating policy on some idealized post-Putin period. Observers should not labour under the impression that a new leader would necessarily be more pro-Western or easily be able successfully to implement a far-reaching liberal reform programme. Nevertheless, there is already considerable change under way in the Russian political elite as a younger generation is being promoted – the military is undergoing its most substantial rotation in a decade, and many new appointments being made to ministerial, governorship and senior civil service positions. Looking to a 'post-Putin' era will create a familiarity with this ongoing evolution in the wider Russian landscape. This would be the basis also for reaching out to this new generation. As Kortunov points out, it is time to think in 'terms of eras and generations, rather than election cycles and bureaucratic squabbles'.[48]

Heading into Different Futures?

The study of Russian futures is a complex subject and one that has, to put it mildly, a chequered past. In the Russia-watching community, futures analysis has often leaned towards increasingly uniform sets of scenarios, and many have incorrectly asserted the unsustainability of Russia's political regime and anticipated Putin's departure. The future is usually painted in bleak colours until a reconciliation with the West and liberal reforms are implemented.[49]

In the broader strategic community, between the end of the Cold War and the outbreak of war in Ukraine, futures analysis hardly mentioned Russia as an active influence in international affairs. When it did feature, it was seen as a power in retreat, if not terminal decline – a view which remains widespread. But since 2014, Russia has once again appeared in governmental strategies. The US analysis *Global Trends 2035*, for instance, points to an increasingly assertive Russia as Moscow 'aspires to restore its great power status through nationalism, military modernisation, nuclear sabre rattling and foreign engagements'. Even so, the report suggests that if the 'Kremlin's tactics falter', Russia will become vulnerable to domestic instability driven by dissatisfied elites; it emphasizes Russia's bleak demographic picture and an undiversified economy, and offers a scenario in which, in the wake of the Indo-Pakistan war of 2028, Putin's successor is 'moving to repair relations with Europe to the benefit of the Russian economy'.[50]

Nevertheless, Russian futures, especially when matched alongside other future studies, are revealing in a number of ways, and help to shape a strategy. Three are worth noting here. First, though futures thinking is difficult – and often proved wrong – a useful understanding of foresight, especially in the short term, is possible. The Canadian government published in 2016 an analysis of short-term 'Russian futures' with a three-year outlook. The study used an analytical framework that eschewed making specific predictions or scenarios, instead examining 'mega-trends' in economics, domestic politics and foreign affairs. These mega-trends indicated the broadly consistent structural context which was unlikely to change substantially across the short period. Within this mega-trend structure, the analysis wove in active and passive 'game changers' – deliberate government policy and the opposition of events respectively – to tailor foresight and understanding of likely developments. Thus, the report was able to offer useful and largely accurate thinking about Russia, even if it went against much orthodoxy and received wisdom.[51]

Second, because most futures analysis blends thinking about themes and geographical regions, it can help to take analysis beyond the current bilateral focus. The UK Ministry of Defence's futures analysis, for instance, runs twenty-seven thematic sets of questions including climate, demography, health, the built environment, transport, automation, artificial intelligence, manufacturing and communications across nine geographical areas.[52]

Third, if it does not mean that disagreements will be overcome, it may illuminate Russian thinking, preparation and action, and offer the means of understanding better how the Euro-Atlantic community and Moscow see the world differently, and thus where competition may arise, and possibly also a broader range of 'common' and 'shared' interests. If both sides see, for instance, increasing competition during the 2020s, the underlying methods of futures analysis often illuminate different emphases. At the same time, there are numerous similar lines in broad-brush futures thinking – including a range of thematic challenges.[53]

While much Euro-Atlantic Russian futures thinking focuses on economic drivers and sustainability, for example, Russian studies often emphasize global trends and shifts, and the need to identify Russia's place in the world, flaws in global governance and the rise of international instability. There is a broad consensus across the Russian policy community about international trends and governance, one that took shape well before the war in Ukraine and the subsequent significant deterioration in relations with the Euro-Atlantic community. Thus the Russian policy community points to 'global shifts that are already underway and will continue regardless of political circumstances'. Disorder will be the primary feature of the international landscape, as a result of a 'triple dissatisfaction' within the leaderships of Western states, in Western societies that are increasingly fearful of globalization, and in leading non-Western states that consider it necessary to develop new rules of the international game that will correspond to the realities of a polycentric world. This dissatisfaction is 'universal in nature, due to deepening inequality, growth in unemployment and the social consequences of migration' – and the lack of an obvious solution illustrates the end of political centrism, the emergence of new forms of ideological struggle and the end of the liberal international order.[54] Many in Moscow are likely to see the developments of the last decade as proving such theories correct.

A second line in Russian futures analysis is the attempt to understand the role of rapid technological change and the impact it will have on society and social stability. This reflects on the possibilities for significant growth of labour productivity but also considerable risks for states that are unable to manage the impact of technological change – such as structural unemployment and marginalization in international affairs. Russian observers and officials often point to the social upheaval and protest movements that emerge at such times of change.[55]

Finally, to illuminate the gaps in futures perspectives, the depiction by a Russian observer of how the world looks in 2037 is worth comparing to that of *Global Trends 2035*. Political and technological developments, combined with climate change, have substantially changed the world. The EU has been broken up following national political upheavals in France, Italy and Germany, and, following the US withdrawal from it in the early 2020s after Europe's failure to support the US during the Taiwan missile crisis, NATO no longer exists. Indeed, the US, led by President Donald Trump Jr, since 2032, has become increasingly isolationist and focused on the defence of its sovereignty in the wake of the '12/25' terrorist attack on San Francisco. Russia and Europe have become partners, cooperating to build the Great Baltic Barrier across the Danish Straits, which prevented the flooding of St Petersburg, the Baltic states, Poland and northern Germany. Domestically, Russia is portrayed as a haven for migrants from South East Asia, and the main issues of the day are cyborg rights.[56]

A 'Contest of Sick Systems'?

What might futures analysis mean for strategy-making? Where might points of competition and shared interest be? As already noted, much Euro-Atlantic foresight thinking emphasizes Russian decline, particularly economic and demographic weakness. They are considered to offer head-winds that will slow Russian material progress as the West 'regains its footing'.[57] This is open to debate, since in the post-Cold War era, though it has remained behind the US and China, Russia has gained ground in terms of national power on the UK, Italy, Germany, France and the US.[58]

At the same time, Gideon Rachman has argued that the power struggles of the twenty-first century are 'more likely to be determined by domestic resilience than external strength', as he highlighted hidden problems, the internal weaknesses and dysfunctionality of the US, China and Russia.[59] This sheds important contextual light on the question of strategy-making. While Russian demographic and economic problems are well known, what is its standing compared to other states? Two points emerge.

The first point is that, despite its broader economic strength and considerably outspending Russia in defence, Europe itself as a region, and the UK within that, face a range of challenges not dissimilar to those faced by Russia. As the European Commission's think tank has noted, Europe's challenges 'show no sign of abating' – economic recovery after 2008 is not felt evenly enough, terrorist attacks threaten major cities and the neighbourhood is destabilized, partly by the largest migration crisis since World War II and partly by the build-up of troops on eastern borders. Climate change, in terms of fresh water, forestry questions and desertification, as well as demographics and economics, pose particular problems.

In terms of demographics, not only does Europe represent a falling share of the world population, but the European population is ageing, and by 2030, Europe will be the oldest region in the world.[60] With persistently low fertility, the European population is set to decline over the next thirty years. While the UK's population will continue to grow, it too will age, with 20.5 per cent of the population over the age of 65 by 2026, resulting in fewer people of working age to support the growing number of those of pension age.[61] The demographic question also includes other features, particularly growing urbanization and increased migration (as a result of climate change and of demographic growth in other parts of the world). These are likely to lead to a range of social and political challenges, including possible increased autonomy for large urban areas, social cohesion and evolving employment and social protection conditions and requirements.

Economically, Europe's relative economic power is forecast to wane, dropping to below 20 per cent of the world's GDP in 2030. The International Monetary Fund (IMF) forecasts that the Euro area will decline from 2.4 per cent real GDP growth in 2018 to 2.0 per cent in 2019 and 1.4 per cent in 2023, with major European countries echoing this: Germany, for instance, declining from 2.5 per cent growth to 1.2 per cent over the same period, and France from 2.1 per cent to 1.6 per cent. The UK's growth is forecast to remain approximately stable – 1.6 per cent in 2018 and in 2023.[62]

The comparative outlook for Russia is similar. Likewise – and perhaps more so – it is challenged by climate change. While this opens up potential advantages, it also creates complications. The opening of the northern sea route, likely to be navigable in the summer months sometime after 2025, may open trade and economic benefits but also may open security challenges; and the impact on northern oil infrastructure – and indeed infrastructure across other parts of Russia – is likely to be negative. If some might argue that the effects of climate change are already being felt in Russia, and infrastructure and state responses are being tested, it also opens questions regarding which other parts of Russia are likely to be affected, whether in terms of agriculture and forestry, or in terms of wildfires, flooding and, given the Soviet ecological inheritance, desertification.[63]

The Russian demographic situation is more complex than is often acknowledged in the Euro-Atlantic debate. The population level suffered catastrophic decline from the late Soviet period through the 1990s and into the 2000s, but the trend was reversed in the late 2000s and early 2010s, with population growth registered. Though it remains a policy priority for the Russian government, over the next decade, the Russian population – with regional variations – will remain broadly stable, thanks to immigration and government health and family policies. But it will be an ageing population, with a growing proportion of people of pension age.[64] Russia is also likely to face the questions posed by growing urbanization, and, as noted, Russian observers and officials are already exploring the consequences of technological change and employment.

Russia's economic performance is uncertain. Some suggest that the forecast for Russia is to remain roughly stable: 1.7 per cent growth in 2018, dipping to 1.5 per cent in 2019 and remaining at that through 2023.[65] If estimates of Russian economic growth recognize that it is likely to be limited to up to 2 per cent, they note that this would be sufficient to sustain current budgetary spending, including on defence. At the same time, Russian data measurements are in the throes of being changed by a new methodology for industrial output, which might give higher figures for growth over the next few years. This means making projections is difficult. Nevertheless, some project that the Russian economy, adjusted for purchasing power parity, will remain one of the major economies – sixth in the world in 2014, it will slip to seventh in 2030, but become the largest in Europe.[66] The role of the state will remain strong, but the economy will have 'archipelago' characteristics, with small pockets of globally competitive sectors. There will also be a shift in the direction of Russian trade, as it, alongside the broader shift in global economic activity, tilts towards East Asia.[67] Though not all priorities will align, these circumstances may broaden the range of shared challenges faced by both the Euro-Atlantic community and Russia.

But in terms of broader Russian foreign and security policy priorities, substantially different futures analyses about the drivers of change and their outcomes make for fewer areas of shared interest. Russian international priorities will reflect a blend of continuity and evolutionary change. Core foreign and security priorities will remain much the same over the next five to ten years, with the Eurasian region retaining its dominance. At the same time, a slow shift in priority will continue away from Europe towards recognizing the importance of the East Asian and Asia-Pacific regions. Though Europe will remain a priority over the next decade, China will gradually match its prominence, and then surpass it.

Most importantly, however, Russia is a country in an ongoing state of mobilization, as its leadership attempts to enhance both its domestic resilience and its strategic deterrence capabilities in anticipation of ever more competition in the 2020s. The sense of an ongoing arms race, looming energy competition as a source of threat, regional conflicts and Moscow's view of the troubled emergence of a new international order – as well as the Euro-Atlantic community's role in international affairs – engender a degree of pessimism in Moscow. The establishment of organizations such as the National Defence Management Centre, with its related system of regional control centres, and the National Guard illustrate the changing defence and security landscape in Russia, and the newly modernized Russian armed forces – substantially re-equipped – will continue to play a central role in the projection of Russian power and the defence of what Moscow sees as its interests, both in Eurasia and, it is likely, beyond. Indeed, increasing Russian activity is already visible not only in Syria, the Arctic and Central Asia, including Afghanistan, but also further afield in the Pacific, Africa, Latin America and Antarctica. The Russian leadership has a global horizon in mind, a 'post-West world', as Lavrov has put it.[68]

The world has changed. Debates will continue about whether Russia is a 'great power'. But a primary feature of the new era that has begun is that Moscow is asserting Russia's place as a ubiquitous and indispensable player in international affairs, often pursuing policies that conflict with the Euro-Atlantic community. Undoubtedly facing many problems, Moscow's view of the world reflects an ambiguous blend of increasing assertion and activity with concern about increasing instability and competition well into the 2020s. Coping with this will require retiring the easy but misleading rhetoric of the twentieth century, and even adapting, updating or completely renewing some cherished and central pillars of the liberal order, and thinking in terms of what is relevant and effective in this new era.

That is not to say that relations with Russia will be easy. Numerous serious disagreements will remain, and new ones are likely to emerge. But dealing with the challenge that Russia poses will require going beyond treating relations in a crisis-management approach and the essentially short-term and tactical nature of the questions that dominate discussion. What is needed is a sustained strategic approach, founded on an updated, sophisticated and nuanced understanding of the nature of the challenge, and a holistic view of Russia and its role in international affairs.

Moscow continues to face serious problems in creating consistent power, especially further afield. But it will not simply disappear or change its policies in accordance with the wishes of the Euro-Atlantic community. To deal with this will require thinking in terms of a new era, and framing the challenges Russia poses not in terms of the rhetoric of the twentieth century, but in the full context of the twenty-first century. This, too, means not just looking through the specific lenses of the wars in Ukraine and Syria, or the intervention in domestic politics, but seeing Russia in holistic terms in a wider geographical context, and that of Moscow's explicit and deliberate attempts to establish Russia as a ubiquitous and indispensable player in international affairs.

Dealing with Russia will involve shaping a new, more sophisticated agenda that establishes a better understanding of Russian regional foreign and security policies, as well as the implications of developing technology, climate change and demography. This new agenda will underpin a broader strategy that incorporates both dialogue and deterrence. Neither dialogue nor deterrence will be easy. Dialogue will require dealing with a Russian leadership that is not inclined to accede to the Euro-Atlantic community's priorities, as well as a cross-cutting, coherent diplomacy and engagement with an emergent generation of Russian officials and politicians. Deterrence will require a much more forward-looking approach that includes a sophisticated grasp of Russian defence and security thinking and the trajectory of Russian capabilities. Sewing these approaches together, and aligning strategic communications with domestic audiences and Russia, will be challenging.

The 'liberal international rules-based order' is by no means finished. But it is not simply how things 'should be' or are destined to be. It will continue both to be challenged by states including Russia, and to evolve. Maintaining the Euro-Atlantic community's driving influence in this evolving order will require considerable effort, including a much more strategic approach to Russia.

Notes

Preface and Acknowledgements

1 'The Return of Old Enemies – How Dangerous is the New East–West Conflict', *Die Welt*, 18 June 2016, http://www.dw.com/en/documentaries-the-return-of-old-enemies-2016-06-18/e-19287458-9798?maca=en; 'World War Three – Inside the War Room', BBC, 3 February 2016, http://www.bbc.co.uk/mediacentre/proginfo/2016/05/inside-the-war-room
2 Luce, E. *The Retreat of Western Liberalism*. London: Little, Brown, 2017. pp. 11–12; Niblett, R. 'Liberalism in Retreat: The Demise of a Dream', *Foreign Affairs*, January/February 2017, https://www.foreignaffairs.com/articles/2016-12-12/liberalism-retreat
3 Zakaria, F. *The Post-American World: And the Rise of the Rest*. London: Allen Lane, 2008; Solana, J. and S. Talbot, 'The Decline of the West and How to Stop it', *New York Times*, 19 October 2016.
4 Haass, R. *World in Disarray: American Foreign Policy and the Crisis of the Old Order*. London: Penguin, 2017. pp. 10–12.
5 Rachman, G. *Easternisation: War and Peace in the Asian Century*. London: Bodley Head, 2016. pp. 3, 247.
6 Allison, G. *Destined for War? Can America and China Escape Thucydides's Trap?* London: Houghton Mifflin, 2017.
7 Bew, J. *Realpolitik: A History*. Oxford: Oxford University Press, 2016. p. 294.

8 Bew, J. 'The Pursuit of World Order in Anglo-American Statecraft', lecture at King's College London, 22 May 2018, https://soundcloud.com/warstudies/inaugural-lecture-professor-john-bew?in=warstudies/sets/events

9 Porter, P. *The Global Village Myth: Distance, War and the Limits of Power*. Washington, DC: Georgetown University Press, 2015. pp. 2–5.

10 Kagan, R. 'The Twilight of the Liberal World Order', Brookings, 24 January 2017, https://www.brookings.edu/research/the-twilight-of-the-liberal-world-order

11 Urban, M. *The Edge: Is the Military Dominance of the West Coming to an End?* London: Abacus, 2015. pp. 39, 143.

12 'Russia Has the Edge Over us in Battle, Army Admits', *The Times*, 10 August 2016.

13 Cited in 'Jim Mattis Warns US Losing Military Edge', *Financial Times*, 19 January 2018.

14 Kirchick, J. *The End of Europe: Dictators, Demagogues, and the Coming Dark Age*. New Haven: Yale University Press, 2017. p. 1. Kirchik's statement about Crimea being the first violent annexation of territory in Europe reflects a widespread view, but overlooks important examples of violence in Europe, including violent annexation such as that in Cyprus in 1974.

15 Kirchick, J. 'Russia's Plot Against the West', *Politico*, 17 March 2017, https://www.politico.eu/article/russia-plot-against-the-west-vladimir-putin-donald-trump-europe

16 McFaul, M. *From Cold War to Hot Peace: The Inside Story of Russia and America*. London: Allen Lane, 2018.

17 'James Clapper on Trump–Russia ties: "My Dashboard Warning Light Was Clearly On"', *NBC News*, 28 May 2017, https://www.nbcnews.com/politics/politics-news/james-clapper-trump-russia-ties-my-dashboard-warning-light-was-n765601

18 Grigas, A. *Beyond Crimea: The New Russian Empire*. New Haven: Yale University Press, 2016. p. 4.

19 Charap, S. and T. Colton, *Everyone Loses: The Ukraine Crisis and the Ruinous Contest for Post-Soviet Eurasia*. London: Adelphi Press, 2017.

20 Mearsheimer, J. 'Why the Ukraine Crisis is the West's Fault: The Liberal Delusions that Provoked Putin', *Foreign Affairs*, September–October 2014, https://www.foreignaffairs.com/articles/russia-fsu/2014-08-18/why-ukraine-crisis-west-s-fault; Cohen, S. 'Cold War Again: Who's Responsible?', *The*

Nation, 1 April 2014, https://www.thenation.com/article/
cold-war-again-whos-responsible

21 Sakwa, R. *Russia Against the Rest: The Post-Cold War Crisis
    of World Order.* Cambridge: Cambridge University Press,
    2017. p. 326; Menon, R. and E. Rumer, *Conflict in Ukraine:
    The Unwinding of the Post-Cold War Order.* London: MIT
    Press, 2015.

22 Schoen, D. *Putin's Master Plan to Destroy Europe, Divide
    NATO, and Restore Russian Power and Global Influence.*
    London: Encounter Books, 2016; Blackwill, R. and P. Gordon,
    *Containing Russia: How to Respond to Moscow's Interven-
    tion in US Democracy and Growing Geopolitical Challenge.*
    Council on Foreign Relations Report, January 2018, https://
    www.cfr.org/report/containing-russia

23 Correspondence with the author, June 2018.

Chapter 1   The Predicament

1 NATO's Wales Summit Declaration, NATO website, 5 Sep-
    tember 2014, http://www.nato.int/cps/en/natohq/official_
    texts_112964.htm; the UK's *National Security Strategy and
    Strategic Defence and Security Review 2015: A Secure and
    Prosperous United Kingdom*, https://www.gov.uk/government/
    uploads/system/uploads/attachment_data/file/478933/52309_
    Cm_9161_NSS_SD_Review_web_only.pdf; and   the   US
    National Defense Strategy, which states that 'long term stra-
    tegic competitions with China and Russia are the principal
    priorities for the department'. *Summary of the 2018 National
    Defense Strategy of the United States of America: Sharpen-
    ing the American Military's Competitive Edge.* Washington,
    DC, 19 January 2018, https://www.defense.gov/Portals/1/
    Documents/pubs/2018-National-Defense-Strategy-Summary.
    pdf. p. 4.

2 Ankara pointed out that they had the right to defend Turkish
    airspace, that the Russian aircraft had violated Turkish air-
    space and had been unresponsive to numerous warnings.
    Medvedev cited in 'Russian Prime Minister Dmitry Medvedev
    Says Turkey's Downing of Su-24 Gave Grounds for War',
    The Independent, 9 December 2015.

3 'The Informational Dimension of Hybrid Warfare: Eastern and Western Perspectives on 21st Century Warfare', seminar at King's College London, 11–12 January 2016; Freedman, L. 'The Limits of Strategy', lecture to LSE IDEAS, 7 April 2016, http://www.lse.ac.uk/IDEAS/Projects/strategy/global_strategies.aspx; Babiracki, P. 'Putin's Post-Modern War with the West', *The Wilson Quarterly*, Winter 2018, which discusses both 'hybrid war' and the Russian interference in US elections.

4 'Is Vladimir Putin Trying to Break up the EU?', BBC News, 30 May 2016, www.bbc.co.uk/news/world-36400924

5 Such accusations are widely discussed in the international media. For convenience, they can be found all together, European and US, in *Putin's Asymmetric Assault on Democracy in Russia and Europe: Implications for US National Security*, a report produced for the Committee on Foreign Relations in the US Senate, and published on 10 January 2018, https://www.foreign.senate.gov/imo/media/doc/FinalRR.pdf. The report seeks to detail the 'weaponisation of civil society, ideology, culture, crime and energy', as well as 'Kremlin interference' in 'semi-consolidated democracies', 'transitional governments' and thirteen 'consolidated democracies' across Europe. These concerns have given rise to numerous political inquiries to establish the extent of Russian interference, such as the UK's Parliamentary Inquiry into Russian influence on the UK's EU referendum, though there are also counter-arguments. 'Russian Tweets on Brexit Were Minimal, Study Shows', *Financial Times*, 19 December 2017.

6 Biden, J. and M. Carpenter, 'How to Stand Up to the Kremlin: Defending Democracy Against its Enemies', *Foreign Affairs*, 5 December 2017.

7 'PM Speech to the Lord Mayor's Banquet', 13 November 2017, https://www.gov.uk/government/speeches/pm-speech-to-the-lord-mayors-banquet-2017

8 'Russia is at War with us, Claims Defence Secretary Gavin Williamson', *The Times*, 9 December 2017; 'Russia Says Britain's Defence Secretary's Claim of Attack Threat Like Something from Monty Python', *The Telegraph*, 26 January 2018; cited in 'Britain has Entered a "New Era of Warfare" with Russian Cyber Attacks, Defence Secretary Warns', *The Independent*, 15 February 2018.

9 Cited in 'NATO Chief: Vladimir Putin "Weaponising" Refugee Crisis to "Break" Europe', *The Daily Telegraph*, 2 March 2016.

10 Shirreff, R. *2017: War with Russia*. London: Coronet, 2016. p. 1. Shirreff's book is presented as a work of fiction, a 'future history'. But the foreword and preface offer the 'non-fiction' views of recently retired senior officers, respectively written by Admiral James Stavridis, NATO SACEUR 2009–13, and Shirreff himself, who served as Stavridis's deputy, March 2011– March 2014. In summer 2015, another study was published also looking at NATO defence of the Baltic states in case of a Russian attack. Hooker, R. D. 'Operation Baltic Fortress, 2016: NATO Defends the Baltic States', *RUSI Journal*, 160:3, June–July 2015, pp. 26–36. Hooker subsequently served in the US National Security Council.

11 'HARDTalk – Ben Hodges, Commanding General, United States Army Europe', BBC News, 20 June 2016, http://www.bbc.co.uk/iplayer/episode/b07gz2f1/hardtalk-ben-hodges-commanding-general-united-states-army-europe

12 'Neighbours Fear "Trojan Horse" as Russia Readies War Games', *Financial Times*, 27 August 2017.

13 'Russia Simulated a War against NATO', *Bild*, 19 December 2017, https://www.bild.de/politik/ausland/bild-international/zapad-2017-english-54233658.bild.html

14 Dunford cited in 'Russia is Greatest Threat to the US, Says Joint Chiefs Chairman Joseph E. Dunford', *Washington Post*, 9 July 2015; 'Dunford: Russia Presents the Greatest Array of Threats', *Seapower*, 29 March 2016, http://www.seapower-magazine.org/stories/20160329-dunford.html

15 'Milley: Russia No. 1 Threat to US', US Army website, 9 November 2015, https://www.army.mil/article/158386/Milley__Russia_No_1_threat_to_US

16 'US Army Chief Sounds Alarm: Military at "High Risk"', *Defense News*, 8 April 2016, http://www.defensenews.com/story/defense/land/army/2016/04/07/army-chief-sounds-alarm-military-high-risk/82763640; Shlapak, D. and M. Johnson, 'Outnumbered, Outranged, and Outgunned: How Russia Defeats NATO', *War on the Rocks* (*WoTR*), 21 April 2016, http://warontherocks.com/2016/04/outnumbered-outranged-and-outgunned-how-russia-defeats-nato

17 Finnish President Sauli Niinisto, 'Press Statements and Answers to Journalists' Questions Following Russo-Finnish

Talks', Website of the Presidential Administration of Russia (WPA), 1 July 2016, http://en.kremlin.ru/events/president/transcripts/52312

18 Sokolsky, R. 'Not Quiet on NATO's Eastern Front: How the Alliance Can De-escalate with Russia', *Foreign Affairs*, 29 June 2016, https://www.foreignaffairs.com/articles/russian-federation/2016-06-29/not-quiet-natos-eastern-front; Saunders, P. 'Russia–NATO: A Classic Security Dilemma', *Valdai Discussion Club*, 12 July 2016, http://valdaiclub.com/news/russia-nato-classic-security-dilemma; Troitsky, M. 'Russia and the West in the European Security Architecture: Clash of Interests or Security Dilemma?', *OSCE Yearbook*, 2015; Rumer, E. *Russia and the Security of Europe*, 30 June 2016, Carnegie Endowment for International Peace, http://carnegieendowment.org/2016/06/30/russia-and-security-of-europe-pub-63990; Sakwa, *Russia Against the Rest*, p. 38.

19 Posen, B. 'The Security Dilemma and Ethnic Conflict', *Survival*, 35, 1, Spring 1993, p. 28; Gat, A. *The Causes of War and the Spread of Peace: But Will War Rebound?* Oxford: Oxford University Press, 2018. p. 249; Jervis, R. *Perception and Misperception in International Politics*. Princeton: Princeton University Press, 1976.

20 Kofman, M. 'Fixing NATO Deterrence in the East or: How I Learned to Stop Worrying and Love NATO's Crushing Defeat by Russia', *WoTR*, 12 May 2016, https://warontherocks.com/2016/05/fixing-nato-deterrence-in-the-east-or-how-i-learned-to-stop-worrying-and-love-natos-crushing-defeat-by-russia

21 Booth, K. and N. Wheeler, *The Security Dilemma: Fear, Cooperation and Trust in World Politics*. London: Palgrave Macmillan, 2008. pp. 4–10.

22 *Russia: Implications for UK Defence and Security*, House of Commons Defence Committee, First Report of 2016–2017. London: HMSO, 2016. p. 6.

23 Interviews with the author, summer and winter 2017.

24 'Press Conference with Secretary Carter at NATO Headquarters, Brussels, Belgium', website of the US Department of Defense, 15 June 2016, https://www.defense.gov/News/Transcripts/Transcript-View/Article/800230/press-conference-with-secretary-carter-at-nato-headquarters-brussels-belgium

25 'US Top Commander in Europe Wants More Resources, Forces, to Deter Russia', *Reuters*, 24 May 2018, https://www.reuters.com/article/us-europe-security/us-top-commander-in-europe-wants-more-resources-forces-to-deter-russia-idUSKCN1IP3IG

26 Booth and Wheeler, *Security Dilemma*, p. 9.

27 Lears, J. 'What We Don't Talk About When We Talk About Russian Hacking', *London Review of Books*, 40:1, 4 January 2018.

28 Shlapak and Johnson, 'Outnumbered, Outranged, and Outgunned', p. 3.

29 Arbatov, A. 'Is a New Cold War Imminent?', *Russia in Global Affairs*, 2, July–September 2007. Like the debate in the West, the 'new Cold War' debate has echoed through the discussion since the mid-2000s, intensifying since 2014, and again with the Skripal affair in 2018. Goltz, A. 'Na Moskovskoi konferentsii po bezopasnosti prezentovali obosnovaniye Kholodnoi Voiny 2.0', *The New Times*, 6 April 2018, https://newtimes.ru/articles/detail/157100

30 'Patrushev predupredil o vozmozhnikh kiberatakakh protiv Rossii', *Tass*, 20 February 2018, http://tass.ru/politika/4975720

31 See the report by Russia's upper house of parliament, the Federation Council, on the protection of sovereignty and the prevention of interference in Russia's internal affairs, presented in October 2017, www.council.gov.ru/media/files/f8SAIXEeNH3T8krO2G1fHZA2W2hTRuMJ.pdf

32 Kampmark, B. 'Bitten by the Bear: The British Council and Russia', *Contemporary Review*, 290:1689, June 2008.

33 Klein, J. 'Space Warfare: Deterrence, Dissuasion and the Law of Armed Conflict', *WoTR*, 30 August 2016, https://warontherocks.com/2016/08/space-warfare-deterrence-dissuasion-and-the-law-of-armed-conflict; Buchanan, B. 'Cyber and Calvinball: What's Missing from Trump's National Security Strategy', *WoTR*, 4 January 2018, https://warontherocks.com/2018/01/cyber-calvinball-whats-missing-trumps-national-security-strategy

Chapter 2   (Mis)interpreting the Russian Threat

1 *National Security Strategy of the United States of America*, December 2017.

2 Westad, O. 'Has a New Cold War Really Begun?', *Foreign Affairs*, 27 March 2018, https://www.foreignaffairs.com/articles/china/2018-03-27/has-new-cold-war-really-begun
3 Haass, R. 'Cold War II', Council on Foreign Relations, 18 February 2018, https://www.cfr.org/article/cold-war-ii
4 'President Trump's Military Strategy Is a Return to the Cold War', *Time*, 19 January 2018, http://time.com/5109551/donald-trump-military-defense-strategy (*Time* also ran a cover story entitled 'Cold War II' in July 2014); 'Trump, Putin and the New Cold War', *Politico*, 22 December 2017, https://www.politico.com/magazine/story/2017/12/22/donald-trump-vladimir-putin-cold-war-216137. There are many such articles; Freedman, L. 'Putin's New Cold War', *New Statesman*, 14 March 2018; Stavridis, J. 'Are we Entering a New Cold War?', *Foreign Policy*, 17 February 2016, http://foreignpolicy.com/2016/02/17/are-we-entering-a-new-cold-war-russia-europe; Smyth, R. 'Is the Growing Crisis with Russia Another Cold War Conflict? Nyet', *The Conversation*, 30 March 2018, https://theconversation.com/is-the-growing-russia-crisis-another-cold-war-conflict-nyet-94093; 'Russia v. The West: Is This a New Cold War?', BBC News, 1 April 2018, http://www.bbc.co.uk/news/world-europe-43581449. Also see the Brookings discussion panel 'Putin's Next Act', 4 April 2018, https://www.brookings.edu/events/putins-next-act
5 'Syria Crisis: UN Chief Says Cold War Is Back', BBC News, 13 April 2018, http://www.bbc.co.uk/news/world-middle-east-43759873
6 'A New Cold War? Russia and the United States, Then and Now', *Foreign Affairs*, April 2018, https://www.foreignaffairs.com/anthologies/2018-04-02/new-cold-war?cid=int-an2&pgtype=hpg&region=br1
7 Legvold, R. *Return to Cold War*. Cambridge: Polity, 2016; Rojansky, M. *George F. Kennan, Containment and the West's Current Russia Problem*, NDC Research Paper, No. 127, January 2016.
8 This section builds on and develops ideas first sketched out in Monaghan, A. *A 'New Cold War'? Abusing History, Misunderstanding Russia*, Chatham House Research Paper, May 2015.
9 'Putin's Speech: Back to Cold War?', BBC News, 10 February 2007, http://news.bbc.co.uk/1/hi/world/europe/6350847.stm;

'Russia Restarts Cold War Patrols', BBC News, 17 August 2007, http://news.bbc.co.uk/1/hi/world/europe/6950986.stm; Sakwa, R. '"New Cold War" or Twenty Years' Crisis? Russia and International Politics', *International Affairs*, 84:2, 2008; Galbreath, D. 'Putin's Russia and the New Cold War: Interpreting Myths and Reality', *Eurasian Studies*, 60:9, 2008.

10 McDermott, R., H. Reisinger and B. Smith-Windsor, 'Cold War Déjà Vu? NATO, Russia and the Crisis in Ukraine', in Lasconjarias, G. and J. Larsen (eds.) *NATO's Response to Hybrid Threats*. Rome: NATO Defence College, 2015; Cohen, S. *Why Cold War Again? How America Lost Post-Soviet Russia*. London: I.B. Tauris, 2018. For discussion of others, see Monaghan, *'New Cold War?'*.

11 Mandelbaum, M. *Mission Failure: America and the World in the Post-Cold War Era*. Oxford: Oxford University Press, 2016.

12 Biden, J. and M. Carpenter, 'How to Stand Up to the Kremlin: Defending Democracy Against its Enemies', *Foreign Affairs*, January/February 2018, https://www.foreignaffairs.com/articles/2017-12-05/how-stand-kremlin

13 'Russian Naval Vessels on Move North of Australia in Lead-Up to G20', *The Guardian*, 12 November 2014.

14 'World Entering Era "More Dangerous Than Cold War" as Russian Power Grows, Former MI6 Boss Warns', *The Independent*, 12 October 2016.

15 May, E. *Lessons from the Past: The Use and Misuse of History in American Foreign Policy*. London: Oxford University Press, 1973. p. xi.

16 Barrass, G. *The Great Cold War: A Journey Through the Hall of Mirrors*. Stanford: Stanford University Press, 2009. p. 379.

17 Freedman, L. 'Frostbitten', *Foreign Affairs*, March/April 2010.

18 Butterfield, H. *Man on His Past*. Cambridge: Cambridge University Press, 1969. p. 23.

19 Freedman, 'Frostbitten'.

20 Kofman, 'Fixing NATO Deterrence'.

21 Officially, eFP forces are described in the Warsaw Summit declaration as 'trigger' forces but they are commonly known as 'tripwire'. The 1950s 'tripwire' strategy was economic but it entailed the danger of almost automatic escalation. It was thus of dubious effectiveness. This underpinned the shift in 1967 to flexible response to defend against a conventional

attack. Luttwak, E. *On the Meaning of Victory. Essays on Strategy*. New York: Simon and Schuster, 1986. p. 165.

22 Mahnken, T. 'Containment: Myth and Metaphor', in Brands, H. and J. Suri (eds.) *The Power of the Past: History and Statecraft*. Washington, DC: Brookings Institution Press, 2016. pp. 133, 138.

23 Kofman, 'Fixing NATO Deterrence'.

24 'Russian Aggression: US Nuclear Missile Commander Says Putin's Actions Echo Those of Nazi Germany in the 1930s', *The Independent*, 22 June 2015.

25 'Minsk "Worse Than Munich", Landsbergis Says', *The Interpreter*, 13 February 2015, http://www.interpretermag.com/minsk-worse-than-munich-landsbergis-says

26 'David Cameron Warns of "Appeasing Putin as We Did Hitler"', *The Guardian*, 2 September 2014.

27 Fettweis, C. 'Misreading the Enemy', *Survival*, 57:5, 2015, p. 164.

28 Chuter, D. 'Munich, of the Blood of Others', in Buffet, C. and D. B. G. Heuser (eds.) *Haunted by History: Myths in International Relations*. Oxford: Berghahn Books, 1998.

29 Record, J. 'The Use and Abuse of History: Munich, Vietnam and Iraq', *Survival*, 49:1, 2007, p. 165.

30 Heuser, B. 'Stalin as Hitler's Successor: Western Interpretations of the Soviet Threat', in Heuser, D. B. G. and R. O'Neill (eds.) *Securing Peace in Europe, 1945–62: Thoughts for the Post Cold War Era*. London: Macmillan, 1992. p. 26.

31 Chuter, 'Munich', pp. 65–7.

32 Bloch, M. *Strange Defeat*. n.p.: Important Books, 2013. pp. 38, 39, 89, 90, 117.

33 Liddell Hart, B. 'French Military Ideas Before the First World War', in Gilbert, M. (ed.) *A Century of Conflict, 1850–1950: Essays for A.J.P. Taylor*. London: Hamish Hamilton, 1966. p. 147.

34 Bloch, *Strange Defeat*, pp. 92–3.

35 Garthoff, R. *Assessing the Adversary*, Washington, DC: Brookings Institution, 1991. p. 51; Barrass, *Great Cold War*, pp. 379–86, 402, 408; Prados, J. *The Soviet Estimate, US Intelligence Analysis and Russian Military Strength*. New York: Dial Press, 1982. pp. 294–5.

36 Ruiz Palmer, D. 'Back to the Future? Russia's Hybrid Warfare, Revolutions in Military Affairs and Cold War Comparisons',

in Lasconjarias and Larsen, *NATO's Response to Hybrid Threats*. Though it is the case that for some, even those who have written of 'Cold War 2.0', 'hybrid war' for example now supersedes the Cold War. Trenin, D. 'Welcome to Cold War II', *Foreign Policy*, 4 March 2014, http://foreignpolicy. com/2014/03/04/welcome-to-cold-war-ii; Trenin, D. 'US Hybrid War Arrives to Replace Cold War', Carnegie Endowment for International Peace, 18 April 2018.

37 Paravincini, G. 'New Chess Game Between West and Russia', *Politico*, 7 November 2016, https://www.politico.eu/article/ natos-struggle-to-close-defence-gaps-against-russia-a2ad

38 Baroudos, C. 'Why NATO Should Fear Russia's A2/AD Capabilities (And How to Respond)', *National Interest*, 21 September 2016, http://nationalinterest.org/blog/the-buzz/why-nato-should-fear-russias-a2-ad-capabilities-how-respond-17776; Kurtdarcan, B. and B. Kayaoglu, 'Russia, Turkey and the Black Sea A2/AD Arms Race', *National Interest*, 5 March 2017, http://nationalinterest.org/feature/russia-turkey-the-black-sea-a2-ad-arms-race-19673; Simon, L. 'Demystifying the A2/AD Buzz', *WoTR*, 4 January 2017, https://waron-therocks.com/2017/01/demystifying-the-a2ad-buzz

39 Raitasalo, J. 'It's Time to Burst the Western A2/AD Bubble', 16 June 2017, http://kkrva.se/en/it-is-time-to-burst-the-western-a2ad-bubble

40 Raitasalo, 'It's Time to Burst the Western A2/AD Bubble'.

41 Tangredi, S. 'A2/AD and Wars of Necessity', *National Interest*, 8 December 2013, http://nationalinterest.org/commentary/ a2-ad-wars-necessity-9524

42 Taylor-Fravel, M. and C. P. Twomey, 'Projecting Strategy: The Myth of Chinese Counter Invention', *Washington Quarterly*, Winter 2015, pp. 173, 179–80.

43 Hoffman, S. 'From Concept to Capability: The People's Republic of China', *CCW Report*, forthcoming.

44 Taylor-Fravel and Twomey, 'Projecting Strategy', p. 181; Kazianis, H. 'America's Air–Sea Battle Concept: An Attempt to Weaken China's A2/AD Strategy', *National Interest*, 22 October 2014, http://nationalinterest.org/blog/the-buzz/ america%E2%80%99s-air-sea-battle-concept-attempt-weaken-china%E2%80%99s-a2-11529

45 Scott, C. 'From Concept to Capability: The Russian Approach to Capability Development', *CCW Report*,

September 2018, http://www.ccw.ox.ac.uk/news/2018/9/19/concept-to-capability-latest-articles-available-on-ccw-website

46 This section draws on and develops Monaghan, A. 'The "War" in Russia's "Hybrid Warfare"', *Parameters*, 45:4, Winter 2015–16.

47 McKew, M. 'The Gerasimov Doctrine', *Politico*, September–October 2017, https://www.politico.com/magazine/story/2017/09/05/gerasimov-doctrine-russia-foreign-policy-215538; 'Valery Gerasimov: The General with a Doctrine for Russia', *Financial Times*, 15 September 2017; Galeotti, M. 'I'm Sorry for Creating the Gerasimov Doctrine', *Foreign Policy*, 5 March 2018, http://foreignpolicy.com/2018/03/05/im-sorry-for-creating-the-gerasimov-doctrine; *International Security and Estonia, 2018*, Tallinn, https://www.valisluureamet.ee/pdf/raport-2018-ENG-web.pdf, p. 47; Warner, M. 'A Fight in the Shadows – the Return of Global Russia', 2 March 2018, https://www.warner.senate.gov/public/index.cfm/2018/3/a-fight-in-the-shadows-the-return-of-global-russia

48 Smith, R. *The Utility of Force: The Art of War in the Modern World*. London: Allen Lane, 2005. p. 4.

49 The centre is intended to strengthen cooperation between the EU and NATO, also delivering expert analysis, developing methodologies and conducting training to enhance capabilities to respond to hybrid threats. It will 'contribute to security in Europe with strengthened cooperation between the EU and NATO, in line with the Joint Communication on countering hybrid threats that was adopted in April 2016', https://www.hybridcoe.fi

50 Mikko Kinnunen was previously the head of the security policy and crisis management unit in the Finnish Ministry of Foreign Affairs. His new role is to work across government to 'identify and counteract hybrid influences'. 'Finland Appoints New Hybrid Threat Ambassador', Yle, 1 April 2018, https://yle.fi/uutiset/osasto/news/finland_appoints_new_hybrid_threat_ambassador/10140750

51 Gerasimov, V. 'Tsennost nauki v predvidennii', *VPK*, 27 February 2013, http://www.vpk-news.ru/articles/14632

52 'Russia Sets up Information Warfare Units – Defence Minister', *Reuters*, 22 February 2017, https://www.reuters.com/article/russia-military-propaganda/russia-sets-up-information-warfare-units-defence-minister-idUSL8N1G753J

53 Hoffman, F. *Conflict in the 21st Century: The Rise of Hybrid Wars*. Arlington: Potomac Institute for Policy Studies, December 2007.

54 Johnson, R. 'Hybrid War and its Counter Measures: A Critique of the Literature', *Small Wars and Insurgencies*, 29:1, 2018. pp. 143, 145.

55 Michaels, J. *The Discourse Trap and the US Military from the War on Terror to the Surge*. London: Palgrave Macmillan, 2013. pp. 1–5.

56 Subject matter specialists have rigorously critiqued the idea of 'Russian hybrid war/Gerasimov Doctrine'. Bartles, C. 'Getting Gerasimov Right', *Military Review*, January–February 2016; Renz, B. and H. Smith, *Russia and Hybrid Warfare: Going Beyond the Label*, Helsinki: Aleksanteri Paper, 1/2016; Charap, S. 'The Ghost of Hybrid Warfare', *Survival*, 7:6, 2016; McDermott, R. 'Does Russia Have a Gerasimov Doctrine?', *Parameters*,46:1, Spring 2016; Giles, K. *Russia's 'New' Tools for Confronting the West: Continuity and Innovation in Moscow's Exercise of Power*, Chatham House Research Paper, March 2016.

57 Ruslan Pukhov, director of Moscow-based Centre for Analysis of Strategies and Technologies, stated 'some in the west seek to inflate him as a strategic visionary. But the truth is that he is a purely military man.' Cited in 'Valery Gerasimov: The General with a Doctrine'.

58 Gerasimov, 'Tsennost nauki v predvidennii'.

59 'U.S. Ambassador: Russia's Hybrid War Against Ukraine Ongoing for 25 Years', UNIAN, 21 December 2016, https://www.unian.info/politics/1690192-us-ambassador-russias-hybrid-war-against-ukraine-ongoing-for-25-years.html; Persson, G. 'The War of the Future: A Conceptual Framework and Practical Conclusions. Essays on Strategic Thought', *Russian Studies Series*, 03/17, NATO Defence College, July 2017.

60 Gerasimov, 'Tsennost nauki v predvidennii'.

61 'Soveshaniye o deistviyakh Vooruzhonnikh Sil Rossii v Sirii', WPA, 17 November 2015, http://kremlin.ru/events/president/news/50714; 'Rasshirennoye zasedaniye kollegi Ministerstva oboroni', WPA, 11 December 2015, http://kremlin.ru/events/president/news/50913

62 Glantz, D. *The Soviet Strategic Offensive in Manchuria, 1945: 'August Storm'*. Abingdon: Frank Cass, 2003. p. 342.

63 Giles, K. 'Russia, Influence and "Hybrid"', in van der Putten, F. et al. (eds.) *Hybrid Conflict: The Roles of Russia, North Korea and China*. Dutch National Network of Safety and Security Analysis, Clingendael Institute, May 2018.

64 Schoen, *Putin's Master Plan, passim.*

65 *Assessing Russian Activities and Intentions in Recent US Elections*, Office of the Director of National Intelligence, ICA 2017-01D, 6 January 2017, https://www.dni.gov/files/documents/ICA_2017_01.pdf. p. iii

66 'If Russia Today is Moscow's Propaganda Arm, it's Not Very Good at its Job', *Washington Post*, 12 January 2017; 'RT's Propaganda is Far Less Influential Than Westerners Fear', *The Economist*, 19 January 2017.

67 Chen, A. 'A So-Called Expert's Uneasy Dive into the Trump–Russia Frenzy', *The New Yorker*, 22 February 2018.

68 Dick, C. J. *Russian Military Reform: Status and Prospects*, CSRC Russia Series, C100, 1998. p. 1.

69 A fine examination of the trials and tribulations of the Russian Armed Forces from 1992 to 2008 can be found in Barabanov, M. 'Russian Military Reform up to the Georgian Conflict', in Howard, C. and R. Pukhov (eds.) *Brothers Armed: Military Aspects of the Crisis in Ukraine*. Minneapolis: East View Press, 2014.

70 Kofman, M. 'From Hammer to Rapier: Russian Military Transformation in Perspective', *CCW Russia Brief 1*, January 2018, http://www.ccw.ox.ac.uk/russia-brief-issue-i

71 Tian, N. et al., *Trends in World Military Expenditure*, SIPRI Fact Sheet, May 2018, p. 2; 'Trump Plans to Ask for $716 Billion for National Defense in 2019 – a Major Increase', *Washington Post*, 26 January 2018.

72 Orwell, G. 'Politics and the English Language', in Packer, G. (ed.) *All Art is Propaganda: Critical Essays*. New York: Mariner Books, 2009. p. 272.

73 Bew, *Realpolitik*, p. 301.

74 Butterfield, H. 'The Dangers of History', in Vaughn, S. (ed.) *Writings on the Uses of History*, Athens: University of Georgia Press, 1985. p. 227.

Chapter 3 From Dialogue to Deterrence

1 'Remarks by High Representative Federica Mogherini at the Press Conference after the Foreign Affairs Council', website of the European Union External Action Service, January 2015, http://eeas.europa.eu/statements-eeas/2015/150119_05_en.htm

2 'Mogherini Suggests Détente with Russia', *Euractiv*, 15 January 2015, http://www.euractiv.com/section/global-europe/news/mogherini-suggests-detente-with-russia

3 Speech by President Jean-Claude Juncker at the 20th St Petersburg International Economic Forum 2016, website of the European Union, 16 June 2016, http://europa.eu/rapid/press-release_SPEECH-16-2234_en.htm

4 Cookson, J. 'Reviving Détente', *The National Interest*, 5 November 2015.

5 Gelb, L. 'Russia and America: Toward a New Détente', *The National Interest*, July–August 2015, http://nationalinterest.org/print/feature/russia-america-toward-new-détente-13077; Ullman, H. 'Needed – a New Détente with Russia', *Atlantic Council*, 2 May 2016, http://www.atlanticcouncil.org/news/in-the-news/ullman-in-upi-needed-a-new-detente-with-russia

6 'President Toomas Hendrik Ilves: Eesti vajab valitsust, kes otsustab ja valitseb', *Eesti Paevaleht*, 22 February 2016, http://epl.delfi.ee/news/eesti/president-toomas-hendrik-ilves-eesti-vajab-valitsust-kes-otsustab-ja-valitseb?id=73742809

7 'Détente with Russia Won't Work This Time', *Wall Street Journal*, 8 June 2015; 'L. Linkyavychyus: Nevyuchennie uroki' ('L. Linkevicius: Unlearned lessons'), 11 December 2015, http://ru.delfi.lt/opinions/comments/llinkyavichyus-nevyuchennye-uroki.d?id=69829200

8 'West Must Engage with Russia, But Can't Be "Business as Usual", Says UK Defence Secretary', *PBS News Hour*, 7 July 2017, https://www.pbs.org/newshour/show/west-must-engage-russia-cant-business-usual-says-u-k-defense-secretary

9 'Meeting of the Valdai International Discussion Club', WPA, 19 September 2013, http://en.kremlin.ru/events/president/news/19243

10 Gomart, T. *EU–Russia Relations: Toward a Way Out of Depression*, CSIS Paper, July 2008; Bordachev, T. 'Georgia, Obama, the Economic Crisis: The Shifting Ground in

Russia–EU Relations', *Russie.NEI.Visions*, 46, January 2010, pp. 4–5, 16–17.

11 Stent, A. *The Limits of Partnership: US–Russian Relations in the 21st Century*. Oxford: Princeton University Press, 2014. pp. ix, x, 82, 255, 256.

12 See Sakwa, R. *Russo–British Relations in the Age of Brexit*, IFRI Report 22, February 2018; Monaghan, A. (ed.) *The UK and Russia: A Troubled Relationship. Part I*, CSRC 07/17, Camberley, 2007; Guseinov, V. and A. Monaghan (eds.) *The UK and Russia: A Troubled Relationship, Part II*, NATO Defence College, August 2009.

13 These included disagreements over the UK's refusal to extradite a number of individuals that Moscow accused of terrorist or criminal activity.

14 *Russia: A New Confrontation?* House of Commons Defence Committee, 10th Report of the Session 2008–2009. HC 276. London: HMSO, 2009.

15 Charap and Colton, *Everyone Loses*, pp. 141–6.

16 'Telephonic Press Briefing with Ambassador Volker, Special Representative for Ukraine Negotiations', State Department website, 29 January 2018, https://www.state.gov/r/pa/ime/useuropeanmediahub/277755.htm; 'Investitsionny forum VTB Kapital "Rossiya Zovyot!"' [VTB Kapital Investment Forum 'Russia Calling!'], WPA, 12 October 2016, http://kremlin.ru/events/president/news/53077

17 Kimmage, M. 'Minsk is Dead! Long Live Minsk?', *WoTR*, 28 December 2017, https://warontherocks.com/2017/12/minsk-dead-long-live-minsk

18 Persson, G. (ed.) *Conventional Arms Control: A Way Forward or Wishful Thinking?*, FOI Research Paper 4586, April 2018. p. 5.

19 Persson, *Conventional Arms Control*, p. 6.

20 'Moscow Does Not Rule Out US's Plans to Secede from INF Treaty, Pledges Instant Mirrored Response', *Interfax*, 19 December 2017.

21 Rumer, E. *A Farewell to Arms … Control*, Carnegie Endowment for International Peace, April 2018. p. 6; Rogov, S. 'Can the US and Russia Find a Path Forward on Arms Control?', *Foreign Affairs*, 22 May 2018, https://www.foreignaffairs.com/articles/russian-federation/2018-05-22/can-us-and-russia-find-path-forward-arms-control

22 The debate about a 'new Yalta' has become a counterpart to the Munich myth. As Marcowitz has pointed out, this is a misunderstanding of what took place at Yalta, and the myth of the division of the world is largely an invention of Charles de Gaulle. Marcowitz, R. 'Yalta, the Myth of the Division of the World', in Buffet and Heuser, *Haunted by History*.

23 'As Syria War Tightens, US and Russia Military Hotlines Humming', *Reuters*, 23 August 2017, https://www.reuters.com/article/us-usa-russia-syria-military-idUSKCN1B32SU

24 'Nachalnik generalogo shtaba VS RF vstretilsya s verkhovnym glavnokomanduyushchim obedinennimy voruzhennymi silami NATO', Russian Ministry of Defence website, 19 April 2018, https://function.mil.ru/news_page/country/more.htm?id=12172028@egNews

25 Naryshkin met US Director of National Intelligence Dan Coats and other US intelligence officials.

26 'Deputy Chief of the Russian General Staff Colonel General Alexander Zhuravlyov had a Meeting with his British Counterpart Gordon Messenger', Russian Ministry of Defence website, 28 February 2017, http://eng.mil.ru/en/news_page/country/more.htm?id=12113164@egNews

27 An example is the Norwegian cooperation to locate a missing Russian helicopter in the Arctic. 'Missing Russian Helicopter Found in Norway Arctic Sea', BBC News, 29 October 2017, https://www.bbc.co.uk/news/world-europe-41794747

28 The Russian space programme has cooperated with the US for some thirty years. Since the US space shuttle programme shut down in 2011, US astronauts rely on Russia to fly to the International Space Station (at $81 million per seat), and in 2017, NASA and Roscosmos announced plans to develop the Deep Space Gateway, part of a long-term plan to send people to Mars. Nonetheless, some suggest that a new space race is taking shape.

29 'Investitsionny forum VTB Kapital'.

30 'Japan–Russia Summit Meeting', Japanese Ministry of Foreign Affairs website, 7 May 2016, https://www.mofa.go.jp/erp/rss/northern/page4e_000427.html

31 'News Conferences Following the Russia–ASEAN Summit', WPA, 20 May 2016, http://en.kremlin.ru/events/president/news/51954

32 Pajon, C. 'Japan–Russia: The Limits of a Strategic Rapprochement', *Russie.NEI.Visions*, 104, October 2017; Kirsten, R. 'Japan–Russia: Abe's Brutal Truth', *The Interpreter*, 4 June 2018, https://www.lowyinstitute.org/the-interpreter/japan-russia-abe-brutal-truth

33 Kireeva, A. *Asymmetry and Development of Russia–Japan Relations*, Russian International Affairs Council, 13 June 2018, http://russiancouncil.ru/en/analytics-and-comments/analytics/asymmetry-of-russia-japan-relations

34 Reynolds, M. 'How to Tame Putin', *Politico*, 2 October 2017, https://www.politico.eu/article/russia-united-states-vladimir-putin-politico-cabinet; Farkas, E. 'How We Can Defeat Putin', *Newsweek*, 20 February 2016, http://www.newsweek.com/vladimir-putin-how-defeat-428755

35 '21st Century Deterrence: Remarks by NATO Deputy Secretary General Alexander Vershbow at the Snow Meeting in Trakai, Lithuania', NATO website, 15 January 2016, https://www.nato.int/cps/en/natohq/opinions_127099.htm

36 Farkas, E. 'Understanding and Deterring Russia: US Policies and Strategies', Testimony Before the House Armed Services Committee, 10 February 2016.

37 Schoen, *Putin's Master Plan*, pp. vii–viii, 123.

38 Schoen, *Putin's Master Plan*, pp. 124–39. Debate over this latter point lasted for years before the Trump administration approved the sale of lethal weapons to Ukraine in December 2017, followed by a similar decision by Canada. The arguments for supplying weapons included giving Kyiv the means with which to defend itself against Russia, and bolstering deterrence by raising the costs to Russia of any renewed offensive. The arguments against included pointing to Ukraine's internal problems contributing not only to Kyiv's own military weakness but also to the likelihood of the weapons finding their way into other hands, whether terrorist or Russian; the risk of the US being drawn deeper into a difficult entanglement; and the fact that Russia could easily match or better the supply of weapons. In spring 2018, 210 Javelin anti-tank missiles and 37 launchers were supplied to Ukraine, though they are kept at a distance from the fighting.

39 Goldberg, J. 'The Obama Doctrine', *The Atlantic*, April 2016, https://www.theatlantic.com/magazine/archive/2016/04/the-obama-doctrine/471525; 'Pence Agrees with Trump:

Calls Putin Stronger Than Obama', *Politico*, 9 August 2016, https://www.politico.com/story/2016/09/mike-pence-agrees-trump-putin-227913

40 Porter, P. 'A Proud Day for Parliament: The Wisdom of Not Bombing Assad', *WoTR*, 30 March 2016, https://warontherocks.com/2016/03/a-proud-day-for-parliament-the-wisdom-of-not-bombing-assad; Hopf, T. *Peripheral Visions*. Ann Arbor: University of Michigan Press, 1995; Press, D. *Calculating Credibility: How Leaders Assess Military Threats*. Ithaca: Cornell University Press, 2005.

41 Ioffe, J. 'How Russia Saw the "Red Line" Crisis', *The Atlantic*, 11 March 2016, https://www.theatlantic.com/international/archive/2016/03/russia-syria-red-line-obama-doctrine-goldberg/473319

42 Wales Summit Declaration.

43 'NATO's Response to Hybrid Threats', NATO website, 26 June 2018, https://www.nato.int/cps/en/natohq/topics_156338.htm

44 'McMaster: Army May Be Outnumbered AND Outgunned in Next War', *Breaking Defense*, 6 April 2016, http://breakingdefense.com/2016/04/mcmaster-army-may-be-outnumbered-and-outgunned-in-next-war

45 'Funding to Deter Russia Reaches $6.5B in FY19 Defense Budget Request', *Defense News*, 12 February 2018; Bugajski, J. and P. Doran, *Black Sea Defended: NATO Responses to Russia's Black Sea Offensive*, Strategic Report No. 2, CEPA, July 2016.

46 'B-2, B-52 Bombers Deploy to Europe for Military Exercises', *Military Times*, 6 June 2015, https://www.militarytimes.com/news/your-military/2015/06/06/b-2-b-52-bombers-deploy-to-europe-for-military-exercises

47 Communication with the author, June 2018.

48 'Nine EU States Sign Off on Joint Military Intervention Force', *The Guardian*, 25 June 2018.

49 Zappe, M. *Efficacy, Not Efficiency: Adjusting NATO's Military Integration*, NDC Research Paper No. 118, August 2015; Braw, E. 'Europe's Readiness Problem', *Foreign Affairs*, 30 November 2017.

50 Correspondence with the author, spring 2018.

51 Speech by Mark Rutte, Prime Minister of the Netherlands, *Bertelsmann Stiftung*, Berlin, 2 March 2018, https://www.government.nl/documents/speeches/2018/03/02/

speech-by-the-prime-minister-of-the-netherlands-mark-rutte-at-the-bertelsmann-stiftung-berlin

52 Connolly, R. *Russia's Response to Sanctions: How Western Economic Statecraft is Reshaping Political Economy in Russia.* Cambridge: Cambridge University Press, 2018.

53 Cooper, J. 'Sanctions Will Hurt Russia's Rearmament Plans', *The Moscow Times*, 12 August 2014.

54 Corbett, A. *Deterring a Nuclear Russia in the 21st Century: Theory and Practice*, NDC Research Report, Rome, NDC, June 2016, p. 1; Rühle, M. 'Deterrence: What it Can (and Cannot) Do', *NATO Review*, Summer 2015, http://www.nato.int/docu/Review/2015/Also-in-2015/deterrence-russia-military/EN/index.htm; Betts, R. 'The Lost Logic of Deterrence', *Foreign Affairs*, March/April 2013, https://www.foreignaffairs.com/articles/united-states/2013-02-11/lost-logic-deterrence

55 Kotkin, S. 'When Stalin Faced Hitler: Who Fooled Whom?', *Foreign Affairs*, November–December 2017, https://www.foreignaffairs.com/articles/russia-fsu/2017-09-19/when-stalin-faced-hitler; Lavrov, A. 'Timeline of Russo–Georgian Hostilities in August 2008', in Pukhov, R. (ed.) *The Tanks of August.* Moscow: CAST, 2010. p. 41.

56 Pollack, J. 'From Lemay to McMaster: The Pentagon's Difficult Relationship with Deterrence', *WoTR*, 29 December 2017.

57 'First European Inspector General Workshop Enhances Alliance', 12 July 2016, www.army.mil/article/171369; 'Polish Officer Jailed for Being a Russian Spy', *Newsweek*, 31 May 2016.

58 Shlapak, D. and M. Johnson, 'Outnumbered, Outranged, and Outgunned: How Russia Defeats NATO', *WoTR*, 21 April 2016, http://warontherocks.com/2016/04/outnumbered-outranged-and-outgunned-how-russia-defeats-nato; Colby, E. and J. Soloman, 'For Peace with Russia, Prepare for War in Europe: NATO and Conventional Deterrence', *WoTR*, 20 April 2016, https://warontherocks.com/2016/04/for-peace-with-russia-prepare-for-war-in-europe-nato-and-conventional-deterrence

59 Shlapak, D. and M. W. Johnson, *Reinforcing Deterrence on NATO's Eastern Flank: War Gaming the Defence of the Baltics*, RAND Report, 2016, pp. 1, 16.

60 Kofman, 'Fixing NATO Deterrence'; Kofman, M. 'The Expensive Pretzel Logic of Deterring Russia by Denial',

WoTR, 23 June 2016, https://warontherocks.com/2016/06/the-expensive-pretzel-logic-of-deterring-russia-by-denial

61 Clem, R. 'Forward Basing NATO Airpower in the Baltics is a Bad Idea', WoTR, 18 April 2016, https://warontherocks.com/2016/04/forward-basing-nato-airpower-in-the-baltics-is-a-bad-idea

62 Lavrov, A. 'Russia's Geopolitical Fears', Moscow Defence Brief 5, 2016, p. 2.

63 'Meeting of the Valdai International Discussion Club', WPA, 24 October 2014, http://en.kremlin.ru/events/president/news/46860; 'Russia May Be Drawn into Resource Wars in Future – Army Chief', RT, 14 February 2013, https://www.rt.com/politics/military-conflict-gerasimov-threat-196; Gerasimov, V. 'Mir na granyakh voiny', VPK, 13 March 2017, https://www.vpk-news.ru/articles/35591; Voennaya Doktrina Rossiiskoi Federatstii, Russian Security Council website, 25 December 2014. http://www.scrf.gov.ru/security/military/document129

64 'Interview to American TV Channel NBC', WPA, 2 March 2018, http://en.kremlin.ru/events/president/news/57027

65 Gerasimov, V. 'Po opytu Syrii', VPK, https://www.vpk-news.ru/articles/29579; Gerasimov, 'Mir na granyakh'.

66 Gerasimov, 'Tsennost nauki v predvidenii'.

67 'Poslaniye Presidenta Federalnomu Sobraniyu', WPA, 1 March 2018, http://kremlin.ru/events/president/news/56957

68 Gerasimov, 'Mir na granyakh'.

69 'Rasshirennoe zasedaniye kollegi Ministerstva oboroni', WPA, 11 December 2015, http://kremlin.ru/events/president/news/50913

70 Cooper, J. 'Russia's State Armament Programme 2018–2027', Russian Studies Series, 01/18, May 2018.

71 Gerasimov, V. 'Sila Velikoi Pobedy', VPK, 11 May 2015; Gareev, M. 'Velikaya Pobeda i sobytiya na Ukraine', Krasnaya Zvezda, 24 April 2014; Gareev, M. 'Voina bez sroka davnosti', VPK, 13 May 2015.

72 '"We Want Historic Dialogue": Macron Says Putin Seeks to Make Russia Great Again', Sputnik International, 5 May 2018, https://sputniknews.com/world/201805061064192929-putin-macron-dialogue-iran-deal

73 Cited in 'Russia-Bashing Must Stop, Says Jean-Claude Juncker', The Guardian, 31 May 2018.

74 'Zasedaniye mezhdunarodnogo diskussionnogo kluba "Valdai"', WPA, 19 October 2017, http://kremlin.ru/events/president/news/55882
75 Interview with the author, May 2018.
76 Kortunov, A. 'A Letter to John: Where Are U.S.–Russia Relations Headed?', Carnegie Moscow Centre, 17 May 2018, https://carnegie.ru/commentary/76336
77 Crankshaw, E. *Putting Up with the Russians*. London: Macmillan, 1984.
78 Goldberg, 'The Obama Doctrine'.
79 Interview with the author, summer 2016.
80 Michaels, J. *Managing 'Simultaneous Deterrence': Avoiding Credibility Failure Amidst Overstretch*, CCW Research Paper, September 2018.

Chapter 4   Dealing with the Russians: Pillars of a Twenty-First-Century Strategy

1 Von Clausewitz, C. *On War*, ed. and trans. Howard, M. and P. Paret. Princeton: Princeton University Press, 1976. pp. 88–9. (emphasis in original).
2 'Russia Will Shoot Down US Missiles Fired at Syria and Retaliate against Launch Sites, Says Russian Ambassador', *The Independent*, 11 April 2018. Ambassador Zasypkin had said he was referring to statements by Putin and Gerasimov, but subsequently this appears to have been in reference to attacks specifically on *Russian* troops.
3 Interview with the author, February 2016.
4 Monaghan, 'New Cold War'?; Sakwa, R. 'A Phony War for Our Times', *Valdai Club*, 16 February 2018, http://valdaiclub.com/a/highlights/a-phony-war-for-our-times; cited in 'Russia Is at War with Us, Claims Defence Secretary Gavin Williamson', *The Times*, 9 December 2017.
5 Selwood, D. 'The Cold War is Over – and the Grey War has Begun', *The Spectator*, 18 April 2018.
6 Barabanov, O. 'A Toxic War Instead of a Cold War', *Valdai Club*, 12 April 2018, http://valdaiclub.com/a/highlights/a-toxic-war-instead-of-a-cold-war

7 Porter, P. 'The Chilcot Inquiry Shows Why the Iraq War Still Matters', *National Interest*, 5 July 2016, http://nationalinterest. org/blog/the-skeptics/the-chilcot-inquiry-shows-why-the-iraq-war-still-matters-16846?page=show

8 For details of the inquiry and the report, see http://webarchive.nationalarchives.gov.uk/20171123123237/http://www.iraqinquiry.org.uk

9 The Chilcot Inquiry endured criticism for the length of time it took to produce the report and its cost, and there is ongoing debate about the extent to which its recommendations have been implemented. 'Government Needs to Act on Key Chilcot Inquiry Finding, Committee Warns', *The Guardian*, 29 May 2018; *Lessons Still To Be Learned from the Chilcot Inquiry: Government Response to the Committee's Tenth Report of Session 2016–17*, 19 December 2017. The Chilcot Report was not the only examination of the UK's involvement in Iraq and Afghanistan: the Butler Review was published in 2004, and the Nimrod Review in 2009, both of which had already begun to influence defence and security thinking.

10 Oborne, P. *Not the Chilcot Report*, London: Head of Zeus, 2016; Ledwidge, F. *Losing Small Wars: British Military Failure in Iraq and Afghanistan*. London: Yale University Press, 2011.

11 These points are laid out in the Ministry of Defence's published response to the Chilcot Report, *The Good Operation: A Handbook for Those Involved in Operational Policy and its Implementation*. London: MoD, January 2018. https://assets. publishing.service.gov.uk/government/uploads/system/uploads/attachment_data/file/674545/TheGoodOperation_WEB.PDF

12 Cornish, P. and K. Donaldson, *2020: World of War*. London: Hodder and Stoughton, 2017. p. 24.

13 McFaul, M. 'Russia as it is: A Grand Strategy for Confronting Putin', *Foreign Affairs*, July/August 2018; Kortunov, A. and O. Oliker, *Roadmap for US–Russia Relations*, CSIS Report, August 2017; Blackwill and Gordon, *Containing Russia*.

14 *Moscow's Gold: Russian Corruption in the UK*. House of Commons Foreign Affairs Committee, 8th Report of the Session 2017–2019, HC 932, London: 21 May 2018, p. 25.

15 Hill, F. 'Towards a Strategy for Dealing with Russia', Brookings, 11 February 2015, https://www.brookings.edu/blog/order-from-chaos/2015/02/11/toward-a-strategy-for-dealing-with-russia

16 McFaul, M. 'The US Needs a Russia Strategy Now More Than Ever', *Foreign Affairs*, 18 July 2018, https://www.foreignaffairs.com/articles/russian-federation/2018-07-18/us-needs-russia-strategy-now-more-ever

17 Gvosdev, N. 'America Must Drop its Delusions about Dealing with Russia', *The National Interest*, 30 March 2018, http://nationalinterest.org/feature/america-must-drop-its-delusions-about-dealing-russia-25147

18 The sanctions cover cyber security, crude oil projects, financial institutions, corruption, human rights abuses, evasion of sanctions, transactions with Russian defence or intelligence sectors, export pipelines, privatisation of state-owned assets by government officials, and arms transfers to Syria. H.R.3364 – 115 Congress, (2017–2018), https://www.congress.gov/bill/115th-congress/house-bill/3364

19 Rumer, E. 'Our National Obsession with Russia Is Preventing Sane Debate', *Los Angeles Times*, 22 January 2018.

20 Petro, N. 'Congress Has Chosen the Wrong Strategy to Deal With Russia', *The National Interest*, 10 December 2017, http://nationalinterest.org/feature/congress-has-chosen-the-wrong-strategy-deal-russia-23584; Ashford, E. 'Why New Russia Sanctions Won't Change Moscow's Behaviour', *Foreign Affairs*, 22 November 2017, https://www.foreignaffairs.com/articles/russia-fsu/2017-11-22/why-new-russia-sanctions-wont-change-moscows-behavior

21 Kofman, M. 'Searching for Strategy in Washington's Competition with Russia', *WoTR*, 30 January 2018, https://warontherocks.com/2018/01/searching-strategy-washingtons-competition-russia

22 'Home Secretary Announces New Counter-Terrorism Strategy', 4 June 2018, https://www.gov.uk/government/speeches/home-secretary-announces-new-counter-terrorism-strategy; 'Director General Andrew Parker Speech to BFV Symposium', 14 May 2018, https://www.mi5.gov.uk/news/director-general-andrew-parker-speech-to-bfv-symposium

23 'Revealed: UK's Push to Strengthen Anti-Russia Alliance', *The Guardian*, 3 May 2018; 'UK to Call for New Russia Response Unit at G7 – Buzzfeed Quoting Johnson', *Reuters*, 7 June 2018, https://uk.reuters.com/article/uk-g7-summit-britain-johnson/uk-to-call-for-new-russia-response-unit-at-g7-buzzfeed-quoting-johnson-idUKKCN1J32WW. The summits turned out to be

difficult opportunities for such an agenda, though – publicly, the G7 and NATO summits were dominated more by President Trump and internal disagreements.

24 Seldon, A. and P. Snowdon, *Cameron at 10: The Inside Story, 2010–2015*. London: William Collins, 2015. pp. 368–70.

25 *The United Kingdom's Relations with Russia: Government Response to the House of Commons Foreign Affairs Committee's Seventh Report of Session 2016–17*. HC332. London: HMSO, 21 September 2017. p. 14. *The National Security Strategy and Strategic Defence and Security Review: A Secure and Prosperous United Kingdom* was also published in 2015.

26 *Russia: Implications for UK Defence and Security*. House of Commons Defence Committee, 1st Report of Session 2016–2017. London: HMSO, 2016. p. 29.

27 Fallon, M. 'Coping with Russia', speech at St Andrews University, 2 February 2017, https://www.gov.uk/government/speeches/coping-with-russia.

28 PM speech to the Lord Mayor's Banquet.

29 Edmunds, T. 'Complexity, Strategy and the National Interest', *International Affairs*, 90:3, May 2014, pp. 525–39.

30 In Bulgakov's book, Voland represents the Devil, who visits Moscow with his entourage and causes havoc. Fallon, 'Coping with Russia'. In his speech, the then Defence Secretary also evinced his dubious grasp of both Russian positions and terminology, such as 'maskirovka'.

31 *Russia: Implications for UK Defence and Security*, 2016, pp. 7, 44.

32 Yalowitz, K. and M. Rojansky, 'The Slow Death of Russian and Eurasian Studies', *The National Interest*, 23 May 2014, http://nationalinterest.org/feature/the-slow-death-russian-eurasian-studies-10516

33 Bershidsky, L. 'Wanted: Russia Experts, No Expertise Required', *Bloomberg*, 20 September 2017. Cited in 'Search for Rationale Behind US Sanctions List', *Financial Times*, 9 April 2018.

34 Frye, T. 'Russia Studies is Thriving, Not Dying', *National Interest*, 3 October 2017.

35 Petro, N. 'Are We Reading Russia Right?', *The Fletcher Forum of World Affairs*, 42:2, Summer 2018.

36 EECAD is the Eastern Europe and Central Asia Directorate. *The United Kingdom's Relations with Russia: Government Response to the House of Commons Foreign Affairs Committee's Seventh Report of Session 2016–17*, p. 14.

37 Sasse, T. and C. Haddon, *How Government Can Work with Academia*, Institute for Government, June 2018, https://www.instituteforgovernment.org.uk/publications/how-government-can-work-academia. pp. 3–4, 8.

38 Tyler, C. 'Wanted: Academics Wise to the Needs of Government', *Nature*, 30 November 2017, https://www.nature.com/articles/d41586-017-077441

39 Dover, R. and M. S. Goodman, 'Impactful Scholarship in Intelligence: A Public Policy Challenge', *British Politics*, 2018, pp. 1–18.

40 Connolly, R. *Towards Self Sufficiency? Economics as a Dimension of Russian Security and the National Security Strategy of the Russian Federation to 2020*, NATO Defence College Russian Studies Series, 01/16, July 2016. p. 1; Mehdiyeva, N. *When Sanctions Bite: Global Export Leadership in a Competitive World and Russia's Energy Strategy to 2035*, NATO Defence College Russian Studies Series, 01/17, February 2017. p. 7.

41 Echoing the situation in the UK, there is more expertise in the Russian private sector. Two examples of Russian research on British politics are Evgeny Minchenko of Minchenko Consulting, and Alexei Gromyko, Director of the Institute of Europe of the Russian Academy of Sciences. Minchenko, E. (ed.) *Kak vyigryvayut vybory v SShA, Velikobritanii i evrosoyuze: Analyz politicheskykh tekhnologii*. Moscow: ISEPI, 2015; Gromyko, A. and E. Ananyeva, *The Current State of Russia–United Kingdom Relations*, Russian International Affairs Council, 8 December 2014. On military questions, Savchenko, E. 'Tekushchie tendentsii razvitiya vooruzhonnykh sil Velikobritanii', *Voennaya Mysl'*, No. 6, 2017 (the author is grateful to Kristin ven Bruusgaard for this reference); and the language educational textbook published by the Russian Ministry of Education and Science and Tomsk University for cadets at the Military Training Centre of National Research, Tomsk State University's Institute of Military Education Studying Linguistic Support for Military Activity, Shevchenko, M. et al., *Voenno-Morskie sili Velikobritanii: Uchebnoe posobie*, Tomsk: Tomsk State University, 2016.

42 De Waal, J. *Depending on the Right People: British Political–Military Relations, 2001–10*. Chatham House Research Paper, November 2013, p. 29.

43 *National Security Strategy* and *Strategic Defence and Security Review*, 23 November 2015.

44 Pastukhov, V. 'Personalno vash', *Ekho Moskvy*, 18 April 2018, https://echo.msk.ru/programs/personalnovash/2186042-echo

45 *Foreign Policy Concept of the Russian Federation*, website of the Russian Foreign Ministry, 18 February 2013, http://www.mid.ru/en/foreign_policy/official_documents/-/asset_publisher/CptICkB6BZ29/content/id/122186

46 Meetings and interviews with the author, 2016.

47 Kortunov, 'A Letter to John'.

48 Kortunov, 'A Letter to John'.

49 Petrov, N. *Putin's Downfall: The Coming Crisis of the Russian Regime*, European Council on Foreign Relations, 19 April 2016; Lipman, M. and N. Petrov (eds.) *Russia 2025: Scenarios for the Russian Future*. London: Palgrave Macmillan, 2013.

50 *Global Trends 2035: Paradox of Progress*. Washington, DC: NIC, January 2017.

51 'Russian Futures to 2018' in *2018 Security Outlook: Risks and Threats*. Ottawa: CSIS, June 2016. A similar approach to futures is visible in EU foresight thinking: Gaub, F. and A. Laban (eds.) *Arab Futures: Three Scenarios for 2025*, Report No. 22, Paris: EUISS, February 2015.

52 Presentation on 'The Global Strategic Trends Programme', NATO website, http://www.act.nato.int/images/stories/events/2012/fc_ipr/160920ws5-ukmod-pres.pdf

53 For discussion of scenarios, see Smith, H. (ed.) *Russia as a Neighbour*. Helsinki: Parliament of Finland, 2014.

54 Barabanov, O. et al. *Global Revolt and Global Order: The Revolutionary Situation in Condition of the World and What to Do About it*. Moscow: Valdai International Discussion Club, February 2017; *Rossiya i mir v 2020 gody: Kontury trevozhnovo budushevo. Geopoliticheski prognoz*, Moscow: Exmo, 2015; Khaustova, N. and O. Glazunov, *Kontury strategicheskoi nestabilnosti XXI veka*, Moscow: URSS, 2013.

55 Remarks by Vladimir Putin at 'Konferentsiya "Vperyod v budushee: rol i mesto Rossii"', WPA, 10 November 2016, http://kremlin.ru/events/president/news/53231; 'Is Society Ready for Future and Technological Change?', 'New Industrialisation: Jobs for People or for Robots?' and 'Alternative 2035: Surrender to Robots or Formalise Fundamental Human Inequality?', http://2035.valdaiclub.com/en

56 Kanareykin, V. 'On the Eve of 2037', Russian International Affairs Council, 23 December 2016, http://russiancouncil.ru/en/analytics-and-comments/analytics/ee-prevoskhoditelstvo-iz-serii-vstrechi-nakanune-2037-g-/?sphrase_id=5074731

57 *Global Trends 2035.*

58 Saradzhyan, S. and N. Abdullaev, *Measuring National Power: Is Putin's Russia in Decline?*, Russia Matters, Belfer Centre Report, May 2018. https://www.russiamatters.org/sites/default/files/media/files/Measuring%20National%20Power.pdf

59 'Russia, America and a Contest of Sick Systems', *Financial Times*, 27 February 2018.

60 *White Paper on the Future of Europe. Reflections and Scenarios for EU27 by 2025*, European Commission, COM (2017) 2025, 1 March 2017, pp. 6, 8.

61 'Overview of the UK Population', Office for National Statistics, 21 July 2017, https://www.ons.gov.uk/peoplepopulationandcommunity/populationandmigration/populationestimates/articles/overviewoftheukpopulation/july2017

62 *World Economic Outlook, April 2018: Cyclical Upswing, Structural Change*, International Monetary Fund, https://www.imf.org/en/Publications/WEO/Issues/2018/03/20/world-economic-outlook-april-2018. p. 241.

63 The author is grateful to Nazrin Mehdiyeva for exchanges on the Russian environment and energy.

64 The Russian population is projected to be 143,786,842 in 2020 and 143,203,543 in 2023, dipping to 141,448,648 in 2028, before a more substantial and accelerated decline in the 2030s. http://worldpopulationreview.com/countries/russia-population

65 *World Economic Outlook, April 2018.* p. 244.

66 *The World in 2050: Will the Shift in Global Economic Power Continue?*, PriceWaterhouseCoopers Report, February 2015, https://www.pwc.com/gx/en/issues/the-economy/assets/world-in-2050-february-2015.pdf, p. 3.

67 The author is grateful to Richard Connolly, Silvana Malle and Julian Cooper for exchanges on the Russian economy.

68 'Foreign Minister Sergey Lavrov's Address and Answers to Questions at the 53rd Munich Security Conference', Munich, 18 February 2017, http://www.mid.ru/en/press_service/minister_speeches/-/asset_publisher/7OvQR5KJWVmR/content/id/2648249

Index